Gilles Lapouge

Pirates and buccaneers

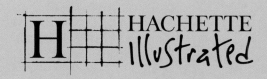

Contents

Juan D'Ulloa et la ville de Vera Cruz, Mexique

Rhodes

5 avril 1851.

Towards the promised sea

They were violent, cruel and not prone to pity. They played for their life with games of chance. They loved bloodshed and the groans of the dying. The injustices of society nauseated them. They believed that the pure, empty, solitary expanses of the sea would protect them from the plagues of history and open up the lost gates of Paradise. They set sail and took arms to exorcise the misfortunes and joys they had experienced on the other side of the sea.

When they put up their camps in their creeks on the wrong side of the world, they lived and let die. Roaring like lions, they threw their grapnels on the stays of galleons, peppering their masts with grapeshot and plunging their daggers into their crews' bellies. And they returned to their lairs to lick their wounds and celebrate.

The gangsters of Chicago and the highwaymen who stripped the rich of their wealth could match the brutality of Blackbeard, Madame Ching, Sir Henry Morgan or Captain Kidd, but they do not merit the title of "pirate". The fact is that, of all the villains who have bloodied history, pirates stand radically and proudly apart: they may have been brigands, but they were brigands of the sea. The sea was their country, their freedom and their prison – it made their adventure irreversible and their departure unrepentant. The sea was the only stage worthy of their hunger and thirst. As Saint-John Perse wrote, "For us the free space of the sea, not ordinary men, blinded by domestic stars."

If I amass a fortune relieving old ladies of their money or robbing stagecoaches, once I have made that fortune I can always retire to my estate and lead the elegant and nostalgic life of a prosperous man of leisure, of a leading citizen, and look after my cats, children and roses.

If I cast off on a doomed ship, however, I have immediately left all hope behind me in the port. I accept that I will never return to the house of men, and that I will die swinging on the end of a rope on Execution Dock in London, or on a tropical beach, probably in my early manhood. I can strut the bridge of a ship, but I have really "burnt my bridges". I have chosen a life with no return and a death with no tomb.

The moment that a young man enlists on a benighted ship is as fateful as the moment when a novice nun becomes the bride of Christ. Like the young girl in the convent, the pirate makes a vow to absence. He erases himself and, by initiating himself in the order of piracy, he dismisses the

PRECEDING DOUBLE PAGE
San Juan d'Ulloa and the city of Vera Cruz

OPPOSITE
Seascape, Eugène Delacroix.

ABOVE
Flag of Algiers.
BELOW
The Spanish Pirate
American caricature, 1898.

OPENING PAGES
Illustrations by Pablo Tillac (details) from *Basque and Bayonnais Corsairs from the 15th to 19th century*, by Pierre Rectoran, 1946.

landscapes of his childhood. He abolishes his friends, his parents and almost his own birth.

From that point on, it is the sea that will decide not only his prosperity, but also his mornings and evenings, his pleasures and his companions. He will remake his life on islands that are so far flung that they only seem to exist in the imagination. To the inhabitants of the hills and dales of England, the pirate had entered the domain of the invisible. He had withdrawn into silence. If he spoke, his words were inaudible, muffled by the wind. The records of his passing were as perishable as the wakes of ships in the blues and blacks of the sea. In mourning for his past yet deprived of a future, the pirate despised both regrets and hopes. This man of nothingness had no other story than the death he dealt out or was dealt, and the death of his brothers in piracy.

The philosopher Gaston Bachelard, who was much given to reveries about water, said that "death is the first navigator". He echoed the funerary dreams of pirates. "Long before the living entrust themselves to the waves" he wrote, "Have they not put their coffin to sea, into the torrent? The coffin, in this mythological hypothesis, would not be the last boat, it would be the first. Death would not be the last journey, it would be the first. For some people who dream deeply, it will be the first true journey". Do pirates form part of these deep dreamers? Their entire epic illustrates Bachelard's beautiful declaration that "the hero of the sea is the hero of death". The pirate would agree with Bachelard, and he would also agree with Heraclitus: "Death is water itself." The waters that bore these ships of revolt lap on the most beautiful and tranquil spots in Europe, Asia, the Americas and Africa – pretty Mediterranean creeks, shores dotted with coconuts in the Caribbean or the Seychelles, the idyllic beaches of India and the crystalline seas of China... These places were not chosen at random:

pirates had a yearning for "heaven on earth" but, as even Moses was unable to attain the "promised land", they headed for the "promised sea". Unfortunately, as all cosmogonies tell us, Heaven and Hell are close to each other, touching and intermingling. Just one tornado is enough to blow the sensual pleasures of the Good Lord into the realms of Satan. Pirates remained unperturbed by these dangers: they made for the lagoons of Genesis and it was just too bad if bliss turned into calamity. This was the punishment and perhaps the joy of the pirate: "Plunge to the bottom of the abyss", wrote Baudelaire, "Hell or Heaven, what does it matter, plunge to the bottom of the unknown to find the new."

This is undoubtedly the explanation for young-sters' fascination with the disastrous tenants of Tortuga, Santo Domingo and the Bahamas. Children love all things tragic and grandiose. On Sundays they go to the beach with their parents and, while they build their sandcastles, they spy out of the corner of their eye the boats that glide by under the clouds; they survey the open sea and see kingdoms that stretch beyond the horizon. They conjure up promontories and gulfs, ham-mocks and uproar, prows splattered with grapeshot, rigging, sea spray, daggers, skulls and crossbones, broken masts, Crusoes and Fridays. At night their dreams are peopled by bandits beyond redemption, striving to start not only society from scratch but also Creation itself.

In 1881, when piracy was well past its heyday, Robert Louis Stevenson was trying to amuse Lloyd Osbourne, the young son of his American lover. "Draw me an island", demanded the child, and Stevenson doodled on a piece of paper. The island contained two havens, a mountain called the Long View, a white rock, a Foremast Hill, a Rum Creek, a Skeleton Isle, three crosses in red ink, and a hideaway full of silver ingots. The cast was set, and that day led to some strange elements appearing in the dreams of children all over the world: patches over the eye, parrots, barrels of rum, lagoons, undertows, scrawls on bits of paper, flags with crossed bones. That very day saw the first entrance onto the stage of several characters, some sinister and some innocent: the young Jim Hawkins, son of an innkeeper in a little English port, an old pirate called Long John Silver whose wooden leg went "click clack" on the planks of the floor, a parrot that shrieked "pieces of eight". Similar images encapsulate the nature of piracy. Let us complete them: in the creeks where they roast their wild pigs, the buccaneers have left other traces scattered behind them – hooks that replaced their hands, chests full of emeralds, blun-derbusses, skeletons of ships eaten by seaweed,

C'EST le **26** mai, si je ne me trompe, deux jours après que notre corvette eut coulé bas, que nous fûmes jetés sur les brisants et notre radeau mis en pièces.

Deux compagnons qui ne savaient pas nager périrent presque aussitôt. Les autres, je veux dire Nicolas Pelsart, le Portugais et moi, gagnèrent à la nage la côte qui se trouvait à un demi-mille environ.

125

Tell me then whether you are the home of the prince of darkness. Tell me... Tell me, ocean (me alone, so as not to sadden those who have still known only illusions), whether the breath of Satan creates tempests that raise the salty waters up to the clouds. You must tell me, because I would rejoice to know Hell so close to man.

Lautréamont

bodies hanging from the prows of kings' ships, gallows, decaying carcasses of tortured victims, glimmering seas, women's breasts, sensual revelry and blood and gold.

For a long time the practice of piracy was nothing more than the gaudy ephemera that captured the imagination not only of children but also of poets, writers, cartoonists and Hollywood directors. Pirate films were one of the glories of Hollywood, and even though they were less common than Westerns, they are no less sublime. Doomed ships have sailed across the screen right from the silent era. In *Captain Blood* Errol Flynn and Olivia de Havilland converted a pair of scoundrels into big-hearted heroes; *The Crimson Pirate* is a master-piece with Burt Lancaster at his best, while *Anne of the Indies* starred Jean Peters as the woman pirate Ann Bonny. After the 1950s the pirate film seemed to have hit the rocks, but it has recently experienced a comeback, thanks to *Pirates of the Caribbean*, starring Johnny Depp.

For the last thirty years pirates have also been opening up new horizons by storming onboard universities. Historians from both Britain and France have examined their dark deeds, brushing the dust off obscure texts written by or about pirates, such as those of the Jesuit Père Labat, the surgeon Oexmelin and, above all, Captain Johnson, a penetrating analyst of piracy now thought to be none other than Daniel Defoe writing under a pseudonym.

Some researchers have dug even deeper. They have discovered that the adventures of these reprobate ships – although they may seem far removed from the larger workings of history – were in fact secretly governed by wars between states, by the conflicting ambitions of European kings, by the life-and-death struggles between the Reformation and Rome or between Spain and England, by gold trafficking, etc.

This work is invaluable, because it has allowed us to form an exact idea of the pirate era. Pirates have entered into the reckoning again: the long erudite arm of history has trapped men whose goal and obsession had been precisely to escape history.

All credit is due to these researchers. In just a few years pirates have become a historical theme, a subject for theses, just like the Hundred Years

War, the price of wheat in the Middle Ages or the art of fortifications in Ming dynasty China. This new dignity is a cause for celebration. Hard cases like Fly or Barbarossa would split their sides laughing at this, but they would also be flattered. Legend still has to resist science, however, so that it does not succumb to the dryness of university research. The history of pirates is also the history of their myth.

All history is at one and the same time a mixture of fable and reality. The *Odyssey*, which was written by "nobody", rules the history of Greece. The death count for the Battle of Bouvines in 1214 was only three, but the noise of its bombardments is still echoing today, and its three corpses have moulded the faces of both France and Europe. The Marne taxis mattered less for the young soldiers they transported than for the literature devoted to them. And now there are doubts as to whether the huge battle of the Catalaunic field, which stopped Attila in his tracks, really took place at all.

If we want to penetrate the mysterious heart of the pirate adventure, we must therefore observe these evildoers in two lights at the same time – that of reality and that of dream. That is why, of all the recent accounts of pirates, the most beautiful and fruitful is that of Michel Le Bris, because it marries the minutiae of historical methods with the demands of myth. The treasure chests of Sir Henry Morgan and Rock the Brazilian are real objects – and this reality is imaginary. The gold coins they contain may come from mines in Peru and New Grenada, but it is nevertheless an alchemical gold, a philosophical gold.

The pirate does not haunt the same space as our society. When his ship appears on the horizon, it is heading for seas far removed from ours. The light that dapples it does not fall from the skies in our history, but it yet conspires with our history, like a parasite accompanying whales or sharks, like a sun trembling in the shadows. Would Europe have the same road network if the exploits of pirates had not cut off sea routes? And would the

"One evening I sat Beauty on my knees. – And I found her bitter.
– And I insulted her.
I have steeled myself against justice.
I have fled. Oh witches, oh misery, oh hatred, it is to you that my treasure has been entrusted! I have succeeded in making all human hope vanish from my spirit. I have made the silent leap of the ferocious beast onto all joy, to strangle it.
I have called for executioners so that I can perish chewing on their gun butts. I have called for scourges so that I can suffocate in sand, in blood. Unhappiness has been my god. I have stretched out in the mud and dried myself in the air of crime. And I have played the fool to the point of madness.
And springtime has brought me the ghastly laugh of the idiot."
Arthur Rimbaud,
A Season in Hell, 1873.

RIGHT
Illustration for *Treasure Island* by
Robert Louis Stevenson,
published by Touret, 1937.

BELOW
Illustration by Louis Marque for
"The Gold-Bug" by
Edgar Allan Poe.

OPPOSITE PAGE
John Silver, illustration from
Characters of romance by
Sir William Nicholson.

English navy have crushed the Armada, would it have put its flag on six continents if Elizabeth I had not subsidised privateers as terrifying and as brilliant as Francis Drake, Cavendish and Hawkins in the 16th century?

In other words, any attempt to describe the grim festival of the freebooters and pirates must listen to the echoes from both sides, from the dream and from the reality. Our voyage will cross the oceans, stopping off in Guyana, the Bahamas, the Seychelles, the China Seas and Madagascar, but it will also take us beyond any atlas into the limbo of history.

And maybe also into the limbo of our own consciousness. The obsessive fears that cast a spell over the waters of the *Revenge* and the *Adventure* are those of our hearts, of the childhood of our hearts: delightful bush schools, defiance of Satan and God, cherished freedoms, blunderbusses and bombards, zigzags through gnawed borders of time and space, heavens and hells, luxurious sins, brotherhoods of reprobates, gallows on beaches and, finally, the abolition of all society. These wild temptations slumber in the depths of all of us – and pirates awaken them. Long after they have deserted the oceans of the Earth, their mouths still babble in the shattered secret of our hearts.

John Silver.

Dionysius, Ulysses and Thucydides

It all began with the first boat, or maybe with the first hollowed trunk, but it was not until Man invented writing that the tracks of predators became discernible in mythology or history, thanks to papyrus, parchments and libraries. These tell us that, since the dawn of history, the "kingdoms of the sea" launched unscrupulous boats all over the Mediterranean. Crete dispatched many crews to the bottom of the sea. Further west, the Tyrrhenians, among them the Etruscans, in their turn pillaged the Crete of Minos. They also attacked the ports of Greece and, from the 8th century BC, the Greek colonies of southern Italy. The historian Strabon recounted how the Greeks' drive into the West was thwarted by these fearsome Tyrrhenian sailors, who had the custom of tying their prisoners face to face with corpses.

The Phoenician pirates were less brutal. Trading softened their rough edges; they made business, not war. One of their boats would stop off in a port with the intention of selling their fine material to the Greek citizens – particularly the female ones. Once their buyers had climbed onboard, they set sail. They would then disembark in another port, where they would sell their prisoners. Some Mediterranean islands, such as Delos, served as markets for these beautiful slaves.

All of the Mediterranean islands, at one time or another, made sacrifices to the art of piracy. Samos was one of the most enterprising of these islands.

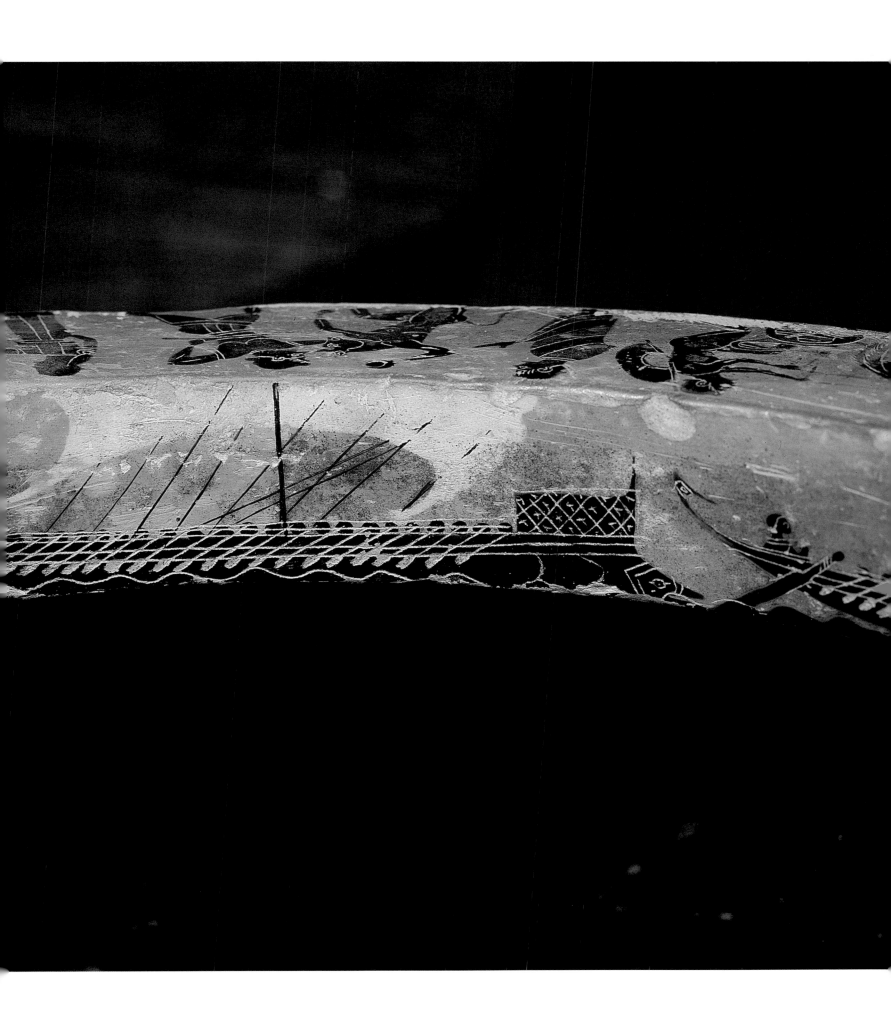

In the 6th century BC its ruler Polycrates (who reigned from 535 to 522 BC) owned more than one hundred boats, including some triremes. He obliterated his rivals from Lesbos and Miletus. He became one of the major figures of his age and made alliances with Cyrus and Cambyses, as well as with the Pharaoh Amasis. As he was prudent, maybe he offered part of his spoils to the sanctuary in Delos! His capital, Samos, was one of the most luxurious cities of the time. Polycrates was a civilised tyrant. He loved art and literature; his court welcomed poets like Anacreon and Ibycos, and the best Athenian doctor, Democedes. The architect Eupalinos rebuilt the monumental temple of Hera and dug through a mountain to create the great subterranean aqueduct that supplied Samos with drinking water.

After a while, however, the Greeks rebelled against the pirates. To ensure the best chances of success, they enlisted skilful and vigorous creatures into their armies: dragons, chimeras, Medusas and lemures. In extreme cases, they called for help from the gods themselves.

One day, a Tyrrhenian crew captured a beautiful young Greek man who was taking a nap on a beach. A fateful error! The young man was Dionysus (Bacchus, the god of the vine, ecstasy and delirium), and he was angry! He decided to take on the form of a lion. This took the Tyrrhenians by surprise; they panicked and jumped into the sea. Dionysus immediately exploited his advantage: he turned his attackers into dolphins and put them to flight. This divine stroke of inspiration did not prove sufficient to pacify the sea, however, and Dionysus did not set a precedent. He would have no imitators. No 17th-century Caribbean pirate would be metamorphosed into a dolphin.

It must be said that Greece had a glowing tradition of piracy. It could even be argued that the *Iliad* and the *Odyssey* are pirate epics – Montesquieu said that all Greeks belonged to this profession! On their longboats adorned with a ram – the "subtle galleys" mentioned by Victor Bérard – hauled by oarsmen or propelled by the wind, they hid in creeks, before pouncing on their dumbfounded enemies. Sometimes they mounted expeditions on

dry land, just as the Caribbean freebooters would do two thousand years later. They surged out of the sea, sacked a port or town and dispersed like a swarm of insects.

Matters were complicated by the fact that piracy was not subject to moral condemnation. The law was vague on this point: the assault of a ship, espe-

beautiful Helen, made forays on the western shores of the Mediterranean.

Achilles followed a similar path and Ulysses, when he returned to Ithaca after ten years of wandering (and probably pillaging), caught sight of Eumeus, his old swineherd, who did not recognise him. Then Ulysses lifted his veil and introduced himself

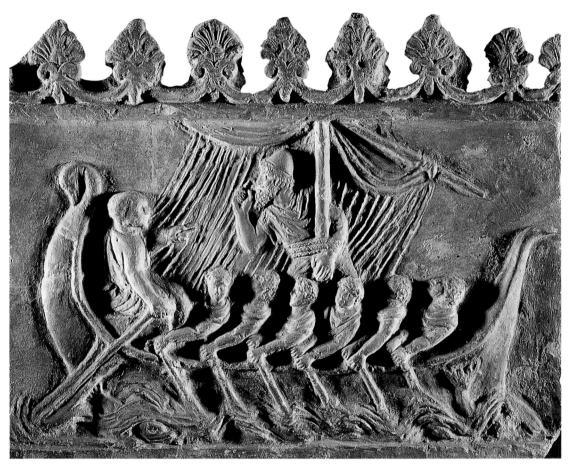

cially that of an enemy, was undertaken with an easy conscience as something resembling hunting, breeding animals, picking fruit or growing crops. In this respect, Homer has left us many descriptions: in the fourth song of the *Iliad*, Agamemnon, who was basically a good prince, imagined the fate awaiting those he conquered: "The vultures will feast on their defenceless flesh and we shall take their women and small children onto our vessels once we have conquered their town." Agamemnon's brother, Menelaus, who was admittedly slightly put out by the debauchery of his

as a pirate. He got somewhat carried away. "What I loved were the oars, the boats, the arrows, the polished javelins. All those tools of death that made others tremble, those were my joy. The gods filled my heart with them." The old swineherd Eumeus was a tolerant man. He mildly cursed the cruelty of pirates, but nevertheless gave the stranger from the sea a warm welcome. Besides, Eumeus was himself reaping the benefits of the trade, as Ithaca was undoubtedly a commercial centre for pirates' booty.

After the fabulous times of Homer, Athens recovered. Mentalities changed: piracy was deemed anathema by the oracle of Thebes and by the Greek chieftains. Pirates, who were marauding all around the Greek territory, were considered despicable.

Writers reflected these developments: in the 5th-4th centuries BC, Xenophon, who was Socrates' pupil, condemned piracy if it was merely for personal gain but turned a blind eye when it was pursued in the context of a war or for the enrichment of a nation. A little earlier, in 424, Thucydides had been appointed a strategist and had commanded an expedition from Athens against Thrace, whose coasts had been infested with brigands from the Chersoneses. He was more severe than Xenophon: he argued that the progress of civilisation was made evident by the disappearance of piracy.

The Athenian triremes served as a police force. They purged the coasts of the island of Skyros and secured Thrace – but pirates are like wasps on honey: they always come back. Crete continued to launch its raids.

The decline of Greece in the 4th century proved a windfall for pirates. An Etolian confederation was formed to bring together the peoples of the Corinth region on the Eolian Sea. The Etolians had bands of brigands who inspired great fear, and the terrified Greek cities made agreements with the confederation to protect themselves from these pirates. Thus the Etolians also increased their sources of support, in all the islands in the Aegean Sea and even on the cost of Iona. It was a world upside down: the Greek islands resisted the advances of the great eastern empires thanks to the protection of the pirate confederation.

There was a similar situation a little later on, when Crete recovered its former spirit of piracy. It should be added that at this time the Cretans were having too many children, resulting in food shortages. So, their chiefs encouraged young people to engage in piracy. The Greek cities again preferred to form alliances with Crete in order to protect themselves against pillaging. Only one city tried to resist the Cretans: the rich island of Rhodes, which needed stability to develop its commerce. At the end of the 3rd century the Rhodeans captured some Cretan pirates, with the support of their Egyptian allies, but, although they continued fighting against them for another fifty years, they were unable to rid the seas of these brigands.

When a child dreams of going to sea or to the Indians, this is an ancient nostalgia, a pre-Babylonian memory that awakens inside him.

Ernst Jünger

Rome and the pirates of Mithridates

Julius Caesar was not yet Emperor. He was just a brilliant and handsome young man, both proud and charismatic. It was the year 78 BC and, as he had been banished by Sulla, he set off to Rhodes, with the intention of studying rhetoric under Apollonius Molon. While in the seas of Caria he fell into the hands of pirates, who demanded a ransom for his release from Rome (where Sulla had just died). Rome offered a generous sum, much to the delight of the pirates, who set about rejoicing their good fortune. Caesar, however, was in no mood for celebrating – he thought he was worth more. He refused to leave his jailers until Rome came up with a ransom worthy of his talent and the prodigious future he foresaw for himself. This episode was just one of the many skirmishes that had been taking place for centuries in the Mediterranean between the bandits that infested its islands and Roman sailors. Some of these islands, such as Corsica and Sardinia, were large, but others were tiny, like the hundreds of rocks off the coast of Illyria that served as a base for extremely skilled navigators like the Istrians, Dalmatians and Liburnians.

Rome faced the challenge that had previously threatened Greece. The Romans, however, were more scrupulous: they favoured the rule of law, clarity, logic and clear distinctions between right and wrong. They decided that piracy could never be considered in the same light as trade. The word went out that pirates were hoodlums who had to be eradicated.

The problem was that the pirates took no notice. The outposts of Crete, Cilicia, Dalmatia and Liguria all revolved round the sea, and when the stocks were low in the Roman markets their customers realised that pirates had struck once again. Even when thousands of their subjects were held by pirates in Crete, the Roman army, whose soldiers were widely dispersed, did not intervene. There came a time, however, when the situation turned decidedly nasty: the brigands of Cilicia came under the wings of the powerful king of Pontus, Mithridates VI Eupator (132–63 BC), who was intent on chasing the Romans out of Asia. Insecurity began to approach the coasts of Italy itself: under the command of Seleucus, known as the "superpirate", the gangs of Mithridates VI reached Ostia, where they sacked the port. The Romans, who were bogged down in the civil war between Marius and Sulla – and who were anyway not particularly fond of the sea – were slow to react, as if they were hypnotised by the dozens of fast, aggressive pirate boats and their insolent crews. All Rome's trading links came under threat and the supply of wheat from Africa was cut off. Rome was in fear of being strangled and the Senate reacted angrily.

In 67 BC full powers were granted to Pompeius, who assembled a huge army of twenty legions and five hundred ships – one hundred and twenty thousand soldiers in all. Pompeius attacked Cilicia and the maze of islets that provided countless

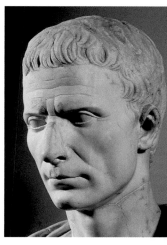

ABOVE
Julius Caesar

If Julius Caesar had been killed by Mithridates, the entire course of history would have changed. Sixteen centuries later a similar fate befell the author of *Don Quixote*, Miguel de Cervantes. After losing his left hand in the Battle of Lepanto, he was captured by pirates who took him to Algiers. There he was sold to a Greek apostate, who found a letter on him from Don John of Austria and therefore reckoned that the one-handed prisoner was a man of influence. He demanded such a high ransom that Cervantes could not be bought back until 1576. His time in captivity later bore fruit, in the form of his plays and novels.

OPPOSITE
Merchant ship, detail of a Roman mosaic.

pirate lairs. Pompeius mercilessly crucified any pirate who refused to surrender. Within forty days Cilicia had been cleansed: four hundred ships were sunk, ten thousand men drowned and a further twenty thousand were captured and sent to work on the land of Rome's agricultural colonies. A few years later, a new offensive by Pompeius succeeded in trapping the pirates' "godfather", the famous Mithridates VI himself, in the Crimea. The cornered king of Pontus took poison but as he had recklessly managed to immunise himself against poison it had little effect and he had to order a soldier to kill him. He bequeathed the French language a verb that would enter the dictionary in 1878: *mithridatiser*, meaning to immunise by accustoming to a poison.

There followed a period of calm. By now, Caesar was in control, ruling with an iron hand. However, after a respite of twenty years, the brigands went back to work – and the irony was that their very talented but very cruel chief, Sextus Pompeius Magnus, was none other than the son of Pompeius the Great, the exterminator of the pirates of Cilicia.

Sextus Pompeius Magnus, who had re-entered the Senate on the death of Caesar, was banished by the second triumvirate. From his base in Sicily, he cut off Rome's communications with the outside world, bringing famine to the city. Octavius Augustus had great difficulty in defeating the pirates but eventually succeeded, thanks to Marcus Agrippa – his loyal friend and subsequent

victor at the Battle of Actium – who defeated Sextus Pompeius at Naulocus in 36 BC. The conquered pirates were recruited into the Roman army en masse and the term *mare nostrum* entered the language.

Three centuries later another danger loomed, in the form of large-scale invasions by Alaric and his Visigoths (which would eventually spell the end for the Romans). Rome trembled and hesitated, and the pirates took advantage by routing the city in 410 and re-embracing their bloody profession. Byzantium took up the sceptre that slid out of the hands of a dying Rome and so took up the fight against the brigands of the sea.

The Byzantine squadrons took to pursuing the elusive Cilicians, with varying degrees of success. Later, with the triumph of Islam, the pillaging

took on a different nature and intensified. In effect, the Arabs, while pursuing their holy wars, also conducted a privateering war that enriched their ports. They sold their Christian prisoners as slaves, and the Byzantines dug into their reserves of gold to buy back their subjects.

In 1204 the Crusaders captured Constantinople, in repugnant style: they massacred, burned and smashed everything in their path. This orgy of blood and gold gave them ideas – they would behave like everybody else, and most particularly the pirates from the Barbary Coast in North Africa. The Christians copied the Muslims by throwing themselves into the slave trade, abducting people here and selling them there. By the end of the Middle Ages this industry was booming: Turks, Moors, Cilicians and Dalmatians would find themselves in Genoa or Venice, passing from one pair of hands to another, from one merchant to another.

The Mediterranean was in chaos, caught up in a vast cycle of pillage, trade, enrichment, exhaustion, vengeance, impoverishment, treason, skirmishes and seizures of ingots. Sicily, Lipari and Malta were studded with disreputable ports but everybody turned a blind eye. Even the Knights of Malta pretended to ignore what was happening as their island was making huge profits.

The Barbary Pirates consolidated their power and struck the Italian coasts. In 1504 Pope Julian II, who was a very severe prince, had to send a precious cargo from Genoa to Civitavecchia and formed a convoy comprising two galleys. En route, the Pope's ships were circled by a small galley that appeared harmless but, through a combination of trickery and violence, it succeeded in capturing the two papal galleys. The assault was led by a stocky man, devoid of pity, with a red beard, and so it was that the first of the Barbarossas burst his way into the history of the Mediterranean.

This Barbarossa is an intriguing character. He was long considered to be a Turkish Muslim, but in fact he was born a Christian (with the name of Arouj), in Mytilene on the island of Lesbos in 1474. He was the son of a Greek potter but he had an adventurous spirit and a desire to be rich, so he converted to Islam and boarded a Turkish pirate ship. His skills made a great impression and he climbed the ranks so quickly that he ended up by

breaking away from his Turkish patrons. He invaded Algeria and subjugated Morocco and Tunisia. Charles V, alerted by the Algerian chieftains, sent ten thousand of his best soldiers to repel Arouj, and he was finally killed in Tlemcen in 1518.

Western Europe rejoiced, but its celebrations were short-lived, as the death of Barbarossa served little purpose. Arouj had a younger brother, equally red-bearded and equally wicked, but with a curious political talent to complement his military prowess. This brother, Khair al-Din (1476–1546), decided to re-enter the orbit of the Turkish

ABOVE
Boat in the port.

Ostia, now situated inland, was once the port of Rome. In the 1st century, the Emperor Claudius built a lake to combat silting on the right bank of the Tiber. This lake, capable of docking two hundred ships, guaranteed Rome's supply of wheat from Egypt. Pirates did not risk entering this maze of quays, guarded by military galleys.

The Barbary Pirates were audacious and cunning. When they made their first appearance in the Mediterranean by capturing two of Pope Julian's galleys, their chief, Barbarossa, presented a remarkable demonstration of his slippery talents. He started by taking one of the galleys by surprise. He then threw all of the Pope's sailors into the hold, having first disguised his own Turkish sailors as Christians. He then placed his sailors in their fancy dress in full view on the deck and, putting his own ship on a towline, headed towards the second papal galley. There, the crew members were exultant but their celebrations were short-lived: Barbarossa's sailors jumped on board, kiledl them and seized their booty.

The Fourth Crusade, instigated by Innocent III, started off with an atrocity: the Crusaders captured Constantinople on 12 April 1204 and carried out a massacre. According to Geoffroi de Villhardouin: "There were so many dead and wounded that it was endless, uncountable". The Christians helped themselves to the holiest relics of Christianity: pieces of the True Cross, thorns from Christ's Crown and bits of the lance that pierced his side. One Crusader managed to filch the Holy Shroud and later took it back with him to Champagne.

Empire. He offered the suzerain of Constantinople the province of Algeria. His calculations were subtle: he did not relinquish any power but he gained the support of the Turks and two thousand janissaries.

Moreover, the Turks granted Khair al-Din a kind of autonomy and he took great advantage of this. The second Barbarossa lived to a ripe old age. When he was eighty years old he married Maria, a pretty young daughter of a Spanish governor whom he captured. Khair al-Din died in 1546.

The events surrounding his funeral bore witness to his support from supernatural powers (common among pirates). According to one chronicle, "his corpse was found four or five times out of the ground in which he had been buried. And it was impossible to keep him in his coffin until a Greek necromancer advised that a black dog should be buried near him. Then Khair al-Din's corpse found peace and no longer disturbed anybody".

The two Barbarossas and the Barbary Pirates have long been subject to debate. Some historians have described them categorically as "pirates". And it is true that, in the beginning, they merited this honour and indignity: they were pirates, just as, for centuries, the Dalmatians, Catalans and Sicilians were, or even those uncontrolled adventurers who

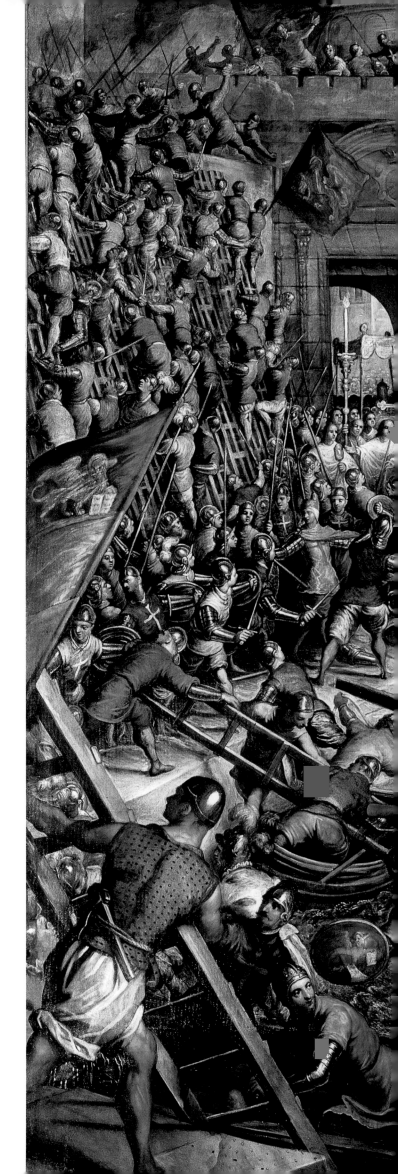

grabbed everything they came across in the vicinity of Malta, with the always unavowed approval of the Knights of Malta. In this period there was nothing unusual about this; on the contrary, it was hard to find any maritime country, city or people who did not practice piracy some time or another

– or at the very least did not make profits from this sullied commerce, as in the case of the Venetians or the Genoese.

Over time, however, and once their success had been consolidated, the Barbary pirates changed their status. Once they had grabbed North Africa they traded in the condition of outlaws for one of Turkish vassals.

The second Barbarossa, Khair al-Din, occupied a position on the borderline between banditry and politics. Did he not sign a treaty with the king of France, Francis I, whose overriding obsession, after the disaster of Pavia, was to wreak havoc on Charles V? So, this rogue found a place in the chess games being conducted in the Mediterranean between Muslims and Christians, and between Christians and Christians, such as the Spaniards, Venetians, Genoese, Turks, French and English.

The Barbary pirates provide an unusual model: a band of outlaws, thieves and murderers, born beyond the horizons of history, in the murky depths of brigandage, who, by means of their immoral actions, gradually became participants in

LEFT
Caricature of a grimacing head, Leonardo da Vinci, ink drawing.

The Barbary pirates made slaves row their galleys. They also used janissaries to fight in battles, and these formed a formidably effective elite corps. However, the Barbary ships were loaded with so many slaves and soldiers that they could not stay long at sea. The pirate chiefs also organised extremely violent lightning raids, after which they withdrew to their bases with the booty.

BELOW
Capture of the harbour by the famous corsair Barbarossa.

RIGHT
Charles V versus Barbarossa in the Battle of Tunis in 1535.

OVERLEAF
Battle of Lepanto, victory of the fleets of Venice, Spain and the Holy See over the Turks, by Andrea Micheli, known as Vicento.

The successors to Barbarossa were fearsome: Dragut settled in Djerba, Mourad occupied the Canary Islands and Ochiali defied Venice by capturing Cyprus. Western Christendom lived in fear. Pope Pius V formed the Holy League. The English, Spaniards, Venetians and Genoese assembled two hundred and eighty ships under the command of a son of Charles V, the brilliant Don John of Austria. At noon on 7 October 1571 the Christians and Turks clashed in Lepanto in a terrible battle. The Christians emerged as victors, leaving thirty thousand Turks dead or wounded. Fifteen thousand Christian prisoners were freed. The Turkish leader, Ali Pacha, was beheaded. The sea was red with blood.

PRESA DELLA CAPITANA DEL FAMOSO CORSARO BARBAROSSA

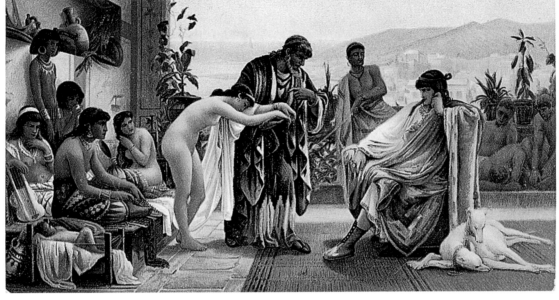

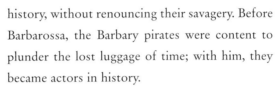

history, without renouncing their savagery. Before
Barbarossa, the Barbary pirates were content to
plunder the lost luggage of time; with him, they
became actors in history.

The descendants of Barbarossa continued to ply
their trade, even after Venice, Pope Pius V,
England and Spain, led by Don John of Austria,
the son of Charles V and the beautiful Barbara
Blomberg , defeated the Turkish fleet at Lepanto
on 7 October 1571.

The memory of the Barbarossas burned for centuries afterwards. Voltaire has left us a witty and
instructive image of these ancient terrors in
Candide: "What surprised me most, said the old
lady when she recounted her capture by the Turks,
was that they put their finger in all of us, in a place
where we others, we women, normally only allow
cannulas to be put. This ceremony seemed very
strange to me: this is how you are judged when
you leave your country. I soon learned that it was
to see whether we had hidden a few diamonds
there: it is an immemorial practice among refined
nations that give on to the sea. I found out that
the gentlemen of the religious knights of Malta
never omit to do this when they capture Turkish
men or women. It is a law of right of people to
whom one has never lowered oneself."

The discovery of America

By adding a new continent to the world, Christopher Columbus cut history into two. Anthropology, theology and metaphysics were all thrown into consternation. Political science reinvented itself with *Utopia* by Thomas More (1478–1535), whose narrator had in effect just returned from the New World. Geography changed its focus – and so did piracy. Horizons broadened and stretched out. The middle of the world changed position and the seas no longer had shores. The Earth became more complicated, and it started to resemble the circle of Hermes Trismegistus, whose centre is everywhere and circumference is nowhere.

The pirates, who were well aware which way the winds of history were blowing – particularly when they whipped up storms – went to seek their fortune in other climes. They replaced the enclosure of the Aegean for the dazzling seascapes of the Caribbean. Idyllic islands and tropical waters attracted these tormented souls, as did the gold and emeralds that the Spanish galleons brought back to Spain and southern Portugal from Peru and Mexico.

Other circumstances encouraged these impulses. Ever since the Renaissance, Europe had been experiencing a slow but inexorable population boom. Its ports abounded in unemployed idlers, who were easily seduced by faraway places and thieving. The ships were perfected. The decks of the old scuttles that had been in use since the early 15th century were relieved of the encumbrance of bombards and culverins. A little later, sailing ships from the North replaced the clumsy and wearisome galleys. These ships were fast, lively and sharp. They were like wasps that stung to death the fat, oafish and over-elaborate Spanish galleons. By the early 16th century everything was in place for the start of the golden age of piracy – the age of the Brothers of the Coast.

Before the buccaneers and freebooters could haunt the creeks of the Caribbean from Cuba and Jamaica to Hispaniola and Barbados, however, European sailors had to make inroads themselves. Three nations stood out: Holland, England and France. They trained, studied, made warm-up runs and got into their stride.

THE NORMANS OF THE NEW WORLD

The French opened the dance of death. They went on the attack. It must be said that Norman sailors had audacity in their blood. They had been sticking their noses everywhere for years. In 1487 or 1488, just before the official discovery of America, one of their captains, Jean Cousin, from Dieppe, reputedly chanced upon the mouth of the Amazon, and Columbus, on his third voyage, had to take refuge in Madeira from French sailors. These had an appalling reputation. They were not only bloodthirsty but also insolent. "Sneeze out the gold", they would say to their prisoners, before cutting off their nose.

SANTA MARIA

SAN·TI·BVRCIO

APRES VN SANGLANT COMBAT ILS
LEVR REPRIRENT LA CARAQVE
DE JVAN DE ITVRRIZA

TILLAC
INV·ET·DEL

ABOVE
Spanish ship from the 16th century.

The galleon, which was the mainstay of the Spanish fleets in the 16th and 17th centuries, succeeded the carack and the caravel. In favourable weather, with trade winds (blowing from east/north-east in the northern hemisphere) in its sails, it could reach speeds of up to 8 knots. Going in the other direction, however, it could only muster a mere 4 knots. It could hold two hundred sailors, was solidly built and very seaworthy, if somewhat clumsy. Despite being heavily armed, it had problems resisting the more nimble ships of the pirates. In the 17th century, the Spanish sailed in convoy to ensure a safe Atlantic crossing. Some convoys numbered up to one hundred ships.

RIGHT
16th-century merchant ship by Hans Holbein the Younger, watercolour, 1525

At the start of the 16th century, Jean Ango, one of Dieppe's most prominent businessmen, began to take an interest in the Portuguese and Spanish ships that visited Brazil, West Africa and the Caribbean. In 1523, in the Azores, one of his captains, the privateer Jean Fleury, seized the Aztec treasure of Moctezuma that the Spaniard Hernan Cortés had intended to give to Charles V. Before long, Fleury would pay for his temerity: he was killed by the Spanish four years later.

Another outstanding Norman was François Le Clerc, popularly known as "Peg Leg". He received a patent from Henry II authorising him to make war in the Americas, and he took good advantage of it. At the head of a thousand sailors, and aided by the fearsome Jacques de Sores, he descended on Puerto Rico in 1553. He ferreted around in small islands like Mona and Saona, and in big ones like Hispaniola, where he pillaged Yaguana (now Port-au-Prince). Then he returned to France, stopping off in Las Palmas, in the Canary Islands. He crops up a few years later in the Protestant cities' uprising against the king in 1562. He even offered his services to Elizabeth I (1558–1603), demanding a pension in return – a demand which

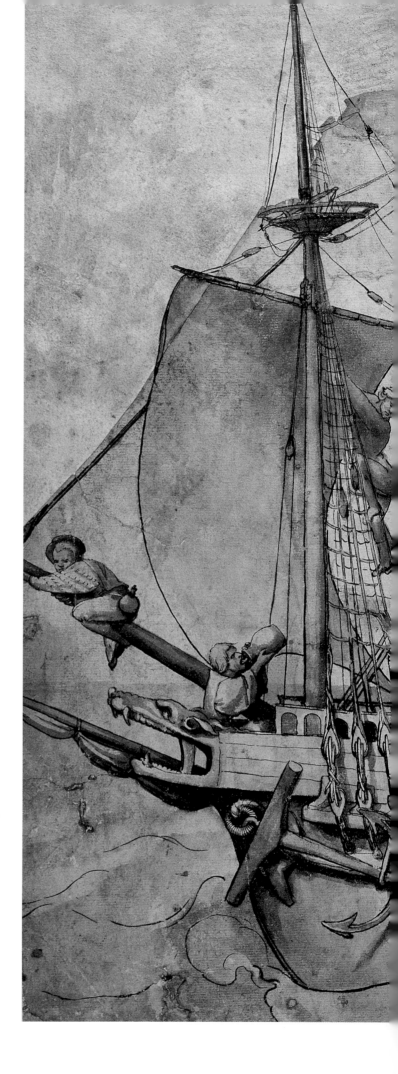

the English queen considered excessive. François Le Clerc was not an easy man to deal with! He went on to the Azores to pester the mythical Spanish "golden fleet" and ended up being killed in a sea battle.

It is apparent that religion played a part in this violence. Europe had been torn apart by Luther and Calvin, and Catholics were set against Huguenots. The major ports of Normandy and La Vendée – La Rochelle, Le Havre and Dieppe – were teeming with Protestants who provided piracy with brilliant leaders and able crews. The first French pirates were Huguenots – Calvinists, not Lutherans, as was often supposed. This affiliation allowed them to follow their instincts without weighing down their consciences. They killed for God and gold at one and the same time. Their courage was exceptional – and so was their cruelty. Of all these captains, one of the most flamboyant was the Norman Jacques de Sores, a fanatical Huguenot. He joined François Le Clerc's band at an early age, before going on to fly with his own,

very blackened wings. On the scale of evil in piracy, de Sores is in the upper reaches, earning himself the title "arch-pirate". In 1554, under orders from François Le Clerc, he took the reputedly impregnable citadel of Santiago in Cuba. The following year he was back in Cuba: this time he sacked Havana. He personally killed 30 Spanish prisoners because he thought it correct to set an example. Furthermore, to rub in the point that God is a Huguenot, he threw parties in the churches. His sailors were exultant: they used the chalices to get drunk, profaned the communion host, smashed the statues and made jesters' costumes out of the priests' chasubles. When they grew tired of insulting the Pope, they set fire to the cathedral.

This type of spree, however, was not sufficient to satisfy the appetite of Jacques de Sores. In 1570 he captured a boat in the sea off La Palma (one of the Canary Islands) that was transporting 39 Jesuits sent by Rome to Brazil. His blood boiled – and the blood of 39 Jesuits was spilled. Father Ignacio de Azevedo, the leader of the mission, was killed

Havana, the capital of Cuba since 1589, was an essential element in Spanish strategy. Situated alongside the Florida Strait and at the entrance to the Gulf of Mexico, it served as a muster station for the Spanish fleet. Galleons took two months to reach Cuba and then arrived back from Porto Bello, Cartagena and Vera Cruz loaded with treasures. The port was basically a magnificent enclosed natural harbour. It was guarded by five forts and the citadel of La Cabana. Privateers and freebooters tried to capture it several times, but a chain barred the entrance and galleons had to wait in the open sea. A number of small boats served as shuttles between the ships and the city.

BELOW RIGHT
An inhabitant of Gibraltar under torture, in *Illustrated history of pirates, corsairs, freebooters, buccaneers, slave traders and brigands of the sea from all ages and all countries* by Jules Trousset, 1891.

and thrown into the sea, entwined with the corpse of his curate. And as Jacques de Sores had not forgotten that, a few years before, Spanish Catholics had massacred Huguenots in Florida, he cut off the hands of the 39 dead Jesuits and threw them into the sea.

That excellent historian of Protestantism, Frank Lestringant, has brought to life this shameful episode. The massacre of La Palma shook Europe. The Jesuits could be relied on to spread the news and make it a matter of pride and tears. In 1571 the *Collection of the most recent letters from the West Indies* – which was translated from Italian into French by one Father Coyssard – was already

painting the martyrdom of the Jesuits with the colours of triumph. Paintings and prints celebrated the event. The Englishman Richard Verstegan was moved to write the *Theatre of the cruelties of the heretics of our times*. Father Louis Richeome denounced the infamy of heretical murderers in *Spiritual painting*. In short, the massacre of La Palma would be fully exploited by the literature and propaganda of the Counter-Reformation.

Frank Lestringant, after a penetrating analysis of the way that both the opposing religions took advantage of the carnage in the Canary Islands in their communications, drew attention to one of the last testimonies to this drama: Paul Claudel's play *The Satin Slipper*. As Lestringant explains, "this series of edifying images reached their conclusion in 1929 in the first scene of *The Satin Slipper* by Paul Claudel. The spectacle of desolation with which the play opens, showing the bridge of a ship strewn with corpses and maimed bodies, is vaguely derived from the massacre of July 1570. In the middle of the Atlantic, equidistant from the New and Old Worlds, a Jesuit priest is dying, tied to, or rather crucified to, the mast of

a Spanish vessel that has been ravaged by pirates. Claudel's memory – and above all his Anglophobia, which had already been perceptible in the farce of *Proteus* – betrayed him on just one point: "Probably the English", says the Announcer of the authors of the massacre. In fact it was committed by Jacques Sore, a privateer of the Queen of Navarre, Jeanne d'Albret, and therefore by French people, although, it must be admitted, rather un-Catholic ones".

HOLLAND AND THE SEA BEGGARS

Holland displayed the same ingredients and the same colours: blood, debauchery, vengeance and religion. Pirates used all their skill and cunning to support the battle waged by the Protestants of William of Orange against the troops of the Catholic occupier, Philip II of Spain.

In 1566, when Philip decided to put a stop to the Dutch people's unruliness, he ordered his legate, the despicable Duke of Alba, to eliminate all the heretics in the country. Resistance was organised immediately. William of Orange – who had been appointed Stadtholder of Holland, Zeeland and Utrecht by Philip II's father, Charles V – led the revolt of the Netherlands against the Spanish, responding in kind to every blow, every torture. He soon won the support of the Dutch privateers, a motley crew of beggars, nobles, aristocrats, adventurers, brigands, amputees, torn ears and gouged eyes who went under the name of "Sea Beggars". William of Orange signed their "letters of marque".

The Catholic leaders, the Duke of Alba and his son, the Duke Don Fadrique, were insatiable in their burning and torturing. Both father and son imprisoned with the implacable zeal that men of religion – be they Protestants or Catholics, Muslims or Jews – espouse when they fight in the name of one sole God – or rather, in the name of one of the five or six sole Gods who have been registered to date. Michel Le Bris provides a blood-curdling detail of their *modus operandi*: the Spanish were very upset when they heard the blasphemies uttered by the Calvinists while they were being tortured. They perfected two methods for remedying this unfortunate situation. The first involved closing the mouth with a vice; the second

DE
AMERICAENSCHE
ZEE-ROOVERS
Behelsende een Partinent
Verhael van alle de Roverye
En Onmenselÿcke Vreet-
heeden die de Engelsche
en Franse Roovers
Tegens de Spanjaerden
in America
Gepleeght
Hebben.

INNO...ENTER

PROPEC...ATIS

t'Amsterdam bÿ JAN ten HOORN, Boeckverkoper
Over het Oude Heerelogement ⊹ 1678

LEFT
Frontispiece of
De Americaensche Zee-Rovers.

OVERLEAF
*Naval victory of the English over
the Spanish Armada in the Armel
Channel, July 1580 (the Spanish
fleet commanded by the Duke
of Medina Sidonia succumb to
the English, commanded by
Francis Drake and
Charles Howard),
by H. Cornelisz Vroom.*

was more technologically advanced: the victim's tongue was put into an iron ring and then burned with a red-hot iron. The tongue would then swell up, its owner finding it most uncomfortable to say anything at all, offensive or otherwise.

The Dutch pirates, the Sea Beggars, responded to such ignominy with equally diabolical fervour. The Catholics and the Protestants combined to bring down upon the country an apocalypse of fire and smoke, sunken boats, drowned and dismembered innocents and rotting corpses.

The Sea Beggars often took refuge in the ports of another Protestant country, England. Dover served as both their base and their supply store. Everything was available on its docks, including prisoners sold as future slaves. The trade was profitable. A noble Spaniard could be bought for up to one hundred pounds in Dover, provided he was well dressed (that was the least that could be asked). Philip II was furious and remonstrated with Queen Elizabeth I, imploring her to renounce her protection of the Sea Beggars.

The Sea Beggars, however, were not prone to obedience. They prospered and their fleet grew to one hundred ships. Their success went to their head and their religious devotion slackened. If they had to choose a religion, they preferred that of money. Under the command of Admiral William Von Lumey Van Der Marck, distinguished by his long hair and huge fingernails – he had sworn to avoid barbers until he had won total victory – they comprised a band of crooks who were so greedy that they made even the English merchants shudder. And Elizabeth I, overwhelmed by the grievances of the Spanish (with whom she was no longer at war), was obliged to turn her wrath against the Sea Beggars. With a heavy heart, she closed the port of Dover to them in March 1572.

Elizabeth's decision did not provide a respite for the Duke of Alba and the Catholics. Once the Sea Beggars were expelled from England, they crossed the English Channel en masse and plunged Flanders and Holland into turmoil. At first the Spanish troops came out on top, bringing hellfire to the city of Malines, spit-roasting babies and hanging men by the penis. Shortly afterwards, at Zutphen, in Gueldre, Don Fadrique, disheartened by the excessive number of people that had to be killed, resolved to drown them in batches of one hundred. Each side, each religion, each sole God reciprocated the ignominies of the other until, in January 1574, the Sea Beggars annihilated the Spanish fleet at Bergen, near Romerswael. The Sea Beggars had chased the mighty Spanish out of Holland.

So, the decision that Elizabeth I took in 1572 to deny the Sea Beggars access to English ports, in particular Dover, paradoxically precipitated the end of Spanish rule over the Netherlands. At the time, however, many people found Elizabeth's decision astonishing. She was not normally given to taking into account the good manners of sailors, especially when they combined the three virtues of being excellent seamen, of sinking Catholic (preferably Spanish) ships and, finally, of raking in loot. It should be pointed out that she was nurturing an ambitious political project. Convinced that England would only be a great power if it won control of the sea, she encouraged her privateers to navigate and trade over long distances, thereby strengthening her fleet and training accomplished sailors and soldiers at the same time, in readiness for the day when she would have to exert her might. With this in mind, she fostered the profession of the privateer.

THE GREAT PRIVATEERS OF ELIZABETH I

Of all the privateers who prospered under Queen Elizabeth I, Francis Drake was the most famous, the most ostentatious and the most reckless. This son of peasants, born in Devon in 1540, took to sea as a boy. He learned how to be a sailor and then branched out into commerce (i.e. pillage).

The Caribbean fascinated the young men of the time. Drake went there three years in a row – 1570, 1571 and 1572. He attacked towns with the help of maroons, rebel slaves who had escaped from the plantations in droves.

There was one town that Drake particularly loved. It was called Nombre de Dios (Name of God), and it contained the "treasure house" in which the Spanish stored the fruits of their larceny. Every year, in the rainy season, the Spanish "golden fleet" loaded up with this booty and took it to Seville. In 1572 Drake and his brigands invaded Nombre de Dios – in vain, as it turned out, as the golden fleet had already passed through and the treasure house was empty. Furious, Drake changed his tactics and decided to intercept the mules that transported Peruvian gold across the Isthmus of Panama. Along with his sidekick John Oxenham he looked for mules – and failed to find them. Oxenham then scoured the Andes on his own and made raids on the Pacific coast. The pickings were good but the Spanish struck back by capturing him in 1578. They took Oxenham to Panama and made him kick his heels for two years before bothering to hang him.

Meanwhile, Drake had been notching up some more exploits. In 1573 he teamed up with another lieutenant, the French geographer Guillaume le Testut, and finally succeeded in catching mules, and the silver they bore. He returned to England with twenty thousand pounds. As this wealth had not been acquired honestly, Drake kept a low profile. It may have been true that Elizabeth was magnanimous, that she was passionate about sailors, the greatness of England and the Protestant religion, but one could never be too sure. Elizabeth was still being threatened by mighty Spain, with which she would shortly be at war. Drake decided it would be better if he was forgotten and set off to fight in Ireland.

In 1577 he re-emerged from out of the shadows. He embarked on a long journey that would last for three years, setting off from Plymouth with

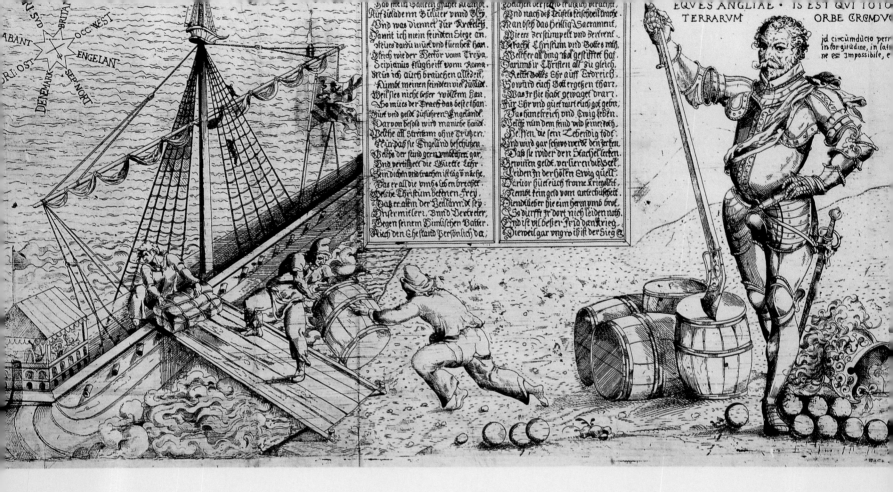

Francis Drake was the greatest sailor of his times, and such an effective pirate that Queen Elizabeth preferred to take on his services on the basis of a commission rather than cut off his head, as the law required. Francis was very similar to Elizabeth, only more extravagant. He was amoral, cold and passionate, a lover of luxury. He went round the world, defeated the Invincible Armada — an extraordinary feat — and founded a colony in virgin America, in an attempt to achieve happiness. His ships carried onboard a painter to record the foreign fauna and flora, a writer, to recount the incidents, exploits, encounters and details, an astrologer, a doctor (obviously) and musicians to provide pleasure. When he was convinced that his second-in-command was hatching treacherous plots, all this allowed him to invite him to dinner on deck, with glassware and silver cutlery, music and stars, before having him executed, much to his regret, as he was anxious to point out. At this time the globe was being assembled. And Shakespeare was writing *Twelfth Night*.

Évelyne Pieiller (*The Almanac of the Frustrated*).

Caca Fogo.

Caca Plata.

LEFT
Drake stopping a Spanish
ship loaded with treasure:
the *Cacafuego*.

RIGHT
The English fleet, under the
command of Drake, captures
the Portuguese town of
Santiago on the island of Cape
Verde, 16 November 1585.

FAR RIGHT
Sir Francis Drake

"The landing of Francis Drake's
Pelican on the Moluccas marked
a discreet beginning that, two
centuries later, would lead to
England becoming the master
of the Indies."
F. Bellec

"England entered the history of
regulated maritime trading in
the style of the Vikings, through
the back door of the attacks
inspired by the thunderous
exploits of Francis Drake."
F. Bellec

five ships and a hundred and sixty sailors. He skirted the coast of Africa, crossed the Atlantic and passed through the Magellan Strait with the intention of taking the Spanish colonies from the rear – and then all those Spanish towns brimming with gold!

The first battles were fierce. Drake captured some insignificant booty but, on 1 March 1579, in the seas of Panama, he fell on a treasure trove, the galleon *Nuestra Señora de la Concepción*, more commonly known as "Cacafuego" (fire shitter). Despite its unappealing nickname, Cacafuego proved to be a cause for celebration: it was crammed with gold, jewellery, precious stones, silver, sugar, chests and coins. It took Drake's sailors six days to load this fortune into the holds of his ship, the *Pelican*.

Drake became an overnight celebrity. The whole of Spanish America knew his name and learned to hate it. He was like a compass rose, reportedly sighted in many places, to the north and south, to the east and west. Drake had the gift of ubiquity, and that was a privilege of devils – it was hardly surprising that the Spanish called him "the dragon".

This highly accomplished sailor chose not to linger: following in the wake of Magellan, he surged into the Pacific, stopped over in the Sundanese islands, went round the Cape of Good Hope and docked in Plymouth to complete his round-the-world trip. He had lost four ships and one hundred and twenty sailors, but he had proved himself to be both a great sailor and a great hoodlum. At the very least he had bagged a lot of gold but, more than that, he had returned alive, whereas the Portuguese sailor Magellan, the only other man who had achieved a similar feat – in 1521, half a century earlier – had died during the voyage. The English considered this seafaring

exploit just as dazzling as the doubloons and ingots packed in the holds of the *Pelican*. Until Drake, the sea had belonged to the Spanish or the Portuguese; now it was the property of the English, and would remain so for a long time to come! Queen Elizabeth could exult: England's destiny would be fulfilled on the high seas!

The city of Plymouth paid homage to the bold explorer-privateer. It spruced itself up and, in a frenzy of excitement, its councillors and burghers, its merchants and ship-owners, its girls – in fact everybody – poured on to the streets. Plymouth drank gallons of beer and other alcohol, and the taverns buzzed with revelry and dancing. Drake was flattered, but he had one concern: what was Elizabeth going to do? The Queen may have been as tough as the great sharks she threw into the sea but she also had arduous political responsibilities, and the Spanish were urging her to act ruthlessly against "the dragon". Mendoza, the Spanish ambassador, was insistent, and there were fears that the Queen would sacrifice Drake for reasons of state and lock him up in the Tower of London – unless she preferred to dismember him. The day of glory or fury arrived. Elizabeth I received Francis Drake for six hours. It is one of the great scenes of history. The two predators saw themselves in each other: the virgin and the adventurer – the woman with the heart of ice and the man with the heart of a wildcat, united by a fistful of doubloons and the scheming inside their heads.

Francis Drake was not only a pitiless privateer, he was also a superb navigator. The nautical observations he made during his expeditions in the South Seas are remarkable for their precision and scientific detail. In 1601 the geographer Richard Hakluyt paid tribute to him in his book *The principal navigations, voyages and discoveries of the English nation*. Four centuries after his death, Sir Francis Drake still serves his country: the drum he took with him on all his expeditions has been lovingly preserved. It has an unusual but practical characteristic: it beats out a mysterious rhythm every time England is in danger.

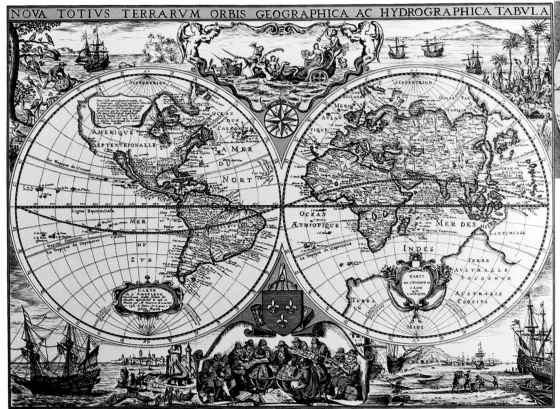

NOVA TOTIVS TERRARVM ORBIS GEOGRAPHICA AC HYDROGRAPHICA TABVLA

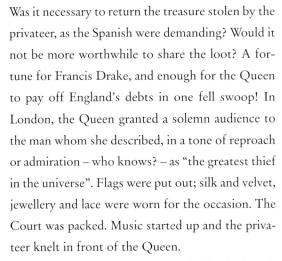

Was it necessary to return the treasure stolen by the privateer, as the Spanish were demanding? Would it not be more worthwhile to share the loot? A fortune for Francis Drake, and enough for the Queen to pay off England's debts in one fell swoop! In London, the Queen granted a solemn audience to the man whom she described, in a tone of reproach or admiration – who knows? – as "the greatest thief in the universe". Flags were put out; silk and velvet, jewellery and lace were worn for the occasion. The Court was packed. Music started up and the privateer knelt in front of the Queen.

Dreamily stroking a golden sword, Elizabeth said: "Captain Drake, the King of Spain has demanded your head. We have a weapon to cut it off with." Silence. "Arise, Sir Francis".

Even Shakespeare could not have done better.

Now Drake was a knight, rolling in gold. He was appointed Mayor of Plymouth but within five years was back in the Caribbean, making failed raids on Santo Domingo and Cartagena.

In 1588 war broke out between Spain and England. Philip II assembled an enormous fleet charged with the mission of landing an army in England and punishing Elizabeth, who had just cut off the head of her Catholic cousin Mary Stuart. The Spanish fleet was nonchalantly given the name "Invincible Armada". Elizabeth made Francis Drake Vice-Admiral of the fleet and, with the help of a few other privateers with skills to match his own (Hawkins, Frobisher, Raleigh, etc.), he sent the Spanish king's ships packing; of the 130 in the Armada, barely 63 straggled back to Spain. This stunning victory marked the beginning of the English navy's reign over the seas of five continents.

Drake had not lost his craving for gold. He set off for the Americas once again but fell sick with a stomach complaint and died off Porto Bello in 1596. He was not the only adventurer to benefit from the bounty of Elizabeth. Anything that served England and the Reformation found favour with

Les pierriers étaient des pièces d'artillerie carrées du coté de la culasse.

Tillac inv. et fe.

LEFT
Attack on a ship by pirates, print by Marks after a drawing by Debelle, in *History of sailors, pirates and corsairs of the ocean and the Mediterranean, including the conquest of Algeria* P. Christian, Paris, 1859.

BELOW
Portrait of Sir Walter Raleigh.

Walter Raleigh (1552–1618) was handsome and knew Latin, Greek and poetry. He assisted William of Orange in his fight against Philip II of Spain in The Netherlands. As Elizabeth I's favourite, he practiced piracy and discovered Virginia, which he named in honour of his "virgin queen". Everything went his way until the day that Elizabeth discovered he was deceiving her. He set off for Guyana, intent on finding El Dorado. On his return to London, he connived in Elizabeth's beheading of one of his rivals, the Earl of Essex. When Elizabeth died, her successor, James I, condemned Raleigh to death in 1603 and imprisoned him in the Tower of London. The sentence was not carried out until 1618, when Sir Walter Raleigh was beheaded.

RIGHT
William Dampier, by Thomas Murray (1663–1734), oil on canvas.

the Virgin Queen. She gathered around her a clique of gifted, if somewhat sinister, sailors who played key roles in the defeat of the Armada. John Hawkins, Drake's uncle, accompanied his nephew on a few forays, but preferred business to war, being the notorious inventor of the slave trade.

The most flamboyant was Walter Raleigh, Elizabeth's erstwhile favourite. Seductive and cruel, he pillaged on a grand scale, participated in the victory over the Armada, published a splendid book (*Report of the truth*), lost his temper with Elizabeth, looked far and wide for El Dorado without success, was condemned to death by Elizabeth's successor then pardoned, made another failed attempt to find El Dorado and finally returned to London, where the king ordered his head to be chopped off.

Thomas Cavendish was an exception to the rule; a sailor who respected his letters of marque and never slid into piracy.

The privateering tradition continued into the next century. Henry Mainwaring was a brigand for four years before settling down as a loyal servant of the Crown in 1617. He also published a book: *Discourse of the beginnings, practices and suppression of pirates*. Later, William Dampier (1652–1715) followed Drake *et al* by combining talent and villainy; he was an excellent sailor with an encyclopaedia for a head. He studied all the plants, animals and stones he came across. He was a cartographer and a writer (*New voyage around the world*). He explored Australia on behalf of the English government but was a hard taskmaster and his crew mutinied. Eventually, he retired. In 1714 he met Alexander Selkirk, the Scottish sailor who had lived from 1704 to 1709 on a desert island in the Juan Fernandez archipelago and was turned into Robinson Crusoe by Daniel Defoe, who also wrote, under the pseudonym of Captain Johnson, the best pirate story of all.

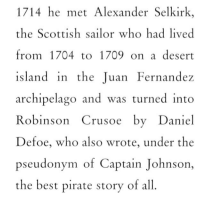

Is a privateer a pirate?

Queen Elizabeth I referred to Francis Drake, with no little affection, as "my pirate". She was right: Sir Francis – like his companions in arms Hawkins, Dampier and Oxenham – was certainly the living embodiment of all the qualities demanded by this loathsome profession. Pirates roamed the seas. They were incomparable sailors of enormous courage. They loved money, women, alcohol, the Caribbean, mules loaded with gold, death, life, daggers and pistols. The word "pity" did not form part of their vocabulary. They killed when necessary, and they killed when not necessary. Finally, they were English; the 16th-century scholar Scaliger was clear that piracy was an English speciality: "Nullus melius piraticum exercent quam Angli". Yes, Elizabeth I certainly had reason to call Drake her pirate, and yet...

And yet, some historians are reluctant to enlist him into the rabble of damnable pirates, and they are not mistaken. The truth is that Elizabeth's brigands, along with those of the kings of France and the Court of Constantinople, were privateers, not pirates. What is the difference? A privateer could be just as bloodthirsty and amoral as a pirate but his deeds enjoyed the protection of the law. He was a mercenary, not a desperado. He had the approval and financial backing of his sovereign. He had a patron, and he could slaughter at will because he had letters of marque from his monarch tucked away in his pocket.

The pirate, however, was made of different stuff

LEFT
Illustration by Berfall, 1849, for
The Red Corsair,
by Fenimore Cooper.

RIGHT
"An American Privateer Taking a British Prize", illustration for "Pennsylvania's Defiance of the United States" by Hampton L. Carson, *Harper's Magazine*, 1908.

OVERLEAF
Illustrations by Pablo Tillac from *Basque and Bayonnais corsairs from the 15th to 19th centuries,* by Pierre Rectoran, 1946.

altogether. He was a loner and his revolt knew no bounds, defying all categorisation. The pirate broke his ties with his family, with his name, with his country, with civilisation, with geography and history, almost with Creation itself. He was a wolf, a creature of darkness and nothingness. He chose to live and die without remorse, without respite and without absolution. He was nobody's plaything – he had no king and no respect for anything. If he behaved despicably, he accepted the price. When he fell, nobody consoled him. He died as he had lived, without redemption. He called on no other witness and no other judge than the loneliness of empty hearts.

The privateers were another matter: the Maltese, French and Corsican sailors who hounded the Ottomans in the 16th and 17th centuries sailed under the flag of the Knights of Saint John of Malta. They killed and pillaged as lustily as anybody, but they did so in a good cause, to wage war

L'abordage se fait en venant reposer l'avant de son navire sur l'arrière de l'ennemi.

Tillac inv. et del.

Philosopher-pirates

Some pirates were of a philosophical bent. The most perceptive of these thinkers was Sam "Black" Bellamy, a Caribbean buccaneer.

One day, he seized one of the King's ships. He captured the captain, and gave him a lesson that was a cross between Bakunin and Marx:

"May God damn you, you are a grovelling dog like all those who accept being governed by the laws that the rich have made for their own security; for those cowardly little dogs do not have the courage to defend in any other way what they have won by their mischief. But, may you be damned altogether: they, as a pile of clever scoundrels, and you, who serve them, as a brainless packet with the heart of a chicken. They revile us, those rogues, although there is only one difference between us and them: they steal from the poor under cover of the law, yes, my God, while we pillage the rich under the sole protection of our courage. Would you not do better to become one of us instead of crawling after those blackguards for a job?

"As for me, I am a free prince and I have as much authority to make war in the whole world as if I had one hundred vessels on the sea or one hundred thousand men in my service, that is what my conscience tells me. But it serves no purpose arguing with such snotty pups who allow their superiors to kick them all along the deck, to their heart's content, and who pin their faith on a pimp of a shepherd, a squab who neither believes nor practises anything he puts in the ridiculous heads of the simpletons he preaches to."

Bartholomew Roberts, the dandy pirate who ravaged the coasts of Guinea, was just as forthright, if somewhat more laconic:

"In a service of honour there is nothing more than hardships and work without reward; but here we breathe only liberty and pleasure without constraint."

against the Infidels, under the patronage of the noble Knights of Malta.

Some historians, such as Hubert Deschamps, have stretched the category of pirate to its limits. They have, for example, bestowed the title on the Vikings who sowed bloodshed and panic throughout Europe, from Sicily to Ireland, during the 9th century. It is certainly true that the Vikings were not very domesticated. Their very name instilled terror: it means "kings of the sea". Their elegant ships – often known as "drakars" but more correctly termed "knarrs" – attacked boats, villages and cities, reaching as far as Russia. Anyone unfortunate enough to fall into the Vikings' path was beheaded with a single blow from their huge axes or double-edged swords. So, they certainly hold their own in any reckoning of cruelty, courage and disdain for human life, but admitting them to the ranks of pirates is something of an indulgence. To earn a diploma for piracy it is not enough to board a ship, sail the high seas, sink ships and hack their crews to bits. This would be a little too easy. To join this illustrious band, these simple pleasures must be complemented by other virtues, other diversions and other duties.

The Vikings lacked these other virtues. They may have been killers who left a bloodbath in their wake, but they were not rebels or outcasts or deserters. Their despair was cut from a different cloth. They loved their society and trusted their rulers; they were soldiers who served the Viking order. At best, they could be called "barbarians of the ocean", borrowing the term that the Greeks used for warriors who were not Greek. It is not hard to find the Vikings detestable, as they were

fierce, wild and bloodthirsty – but they were not pirates.

These distinctions are not futile. The difference between a privateer and a pirate is that the former can go back to living in society whenever he so desires, whereas a true pirate is banished for ever. He has chosen exile in its purest form. He has amputated anything that might add sweetness to the human condition. When he leaves Europe he slams the door behind him and he knows that he will never be able to reopen it, unless he betrays the oath he has made to himself.

Romantic writers were fully aware that the Devil has the best tunes. They loved the idea of the pirate, a haunted creature sworn to unending flight, determined to live in the twilight of death. Leaving aside Robert Louis Stevenson and his masterly *Treasure Island*, also worthy of note are Schiller with *The Robbers*, Walter Scott and his

du 21. au 22 floréal.

Midi j'ai observé de latitude Sud ...

...9. route couru corrigé le Sud 1/4 Est, Chemin Cinglé .... 117 miles

longitude estimé orientale ..... M ... de paris ....

du 22. au 23. floréal.

pendant ces 24 heures le tems a été fort beau, le vent a varié de L'Est au N.E par le nord, on a fait route au Sud toutes voiles dehors, la mer belle, on a changé

...O.18. un petit hunier, a midi j'ai observé de latitude Sud .... 25.° 6;

Route couru le S.S.E. 5° Sud, Chemin Cinglé .... 94 miles

Longitude estimé orientale M. P. .... 54.° 58;

du 23. au 24. floréal

le tems beau joli frais, la mer belle, les vents ont varié dans les vingt quatre

heures du N.E, a O.N.O, on a fait route toutes voiles dehors au S.S.E, du compas.

W.on N.O.18, a midi j'ai observé de latitude Sud .... 26.° 22;

la route m'a valu Corrigé le S.E, 3° E. Chemin Cinglé ..... 114 miles

longitude Orientale M. P. estimé .... 56.° 32,

du 24 au 25. floréal.

le tems assez beau, le vent soufflant du S.O, variable au Sud, joli frais.

gouvernant sous toutes voiles au plus près du vent tribord amures. la mer

houleuse du S.E. a deux heures du matin le vent ayant sauté au S.O,

W.on N.O.18 on a pris babord amures vent devant, le vent ensuite repris au Sud, continué

le même bord, a midi j'ai observé de latitude Sud .... 26.° 50;

la route des 24 h.res m'a valu Corrigé L'E.S.E; Chemin id. — 70. miles ....

Longitude estimé Orientale M. Paris .... 57.° 44;

pendant ces 24. h.res les vents ont regnez du S.E. variable au S.O. Bon frais la
grosse. Cinglant au p.s près durent Câbord amure sous les quatre voiles mej...

à Midi j'ai observée de latitude Sud .... 28° 2;

19° — Route Courru Corrigé le S.O, 4¾ Sud, Chemin Cinglé. 96. miles

longitude arrivé orientale M. paris .... 56.° 33;

Du 26. au 27. floréal

beau tems petit Frais, de l'E, S.E, variable au Sud, la mer houleuse du S.
Cinglant toutes voiles dehors au plus près durent Câbord amure; a 10 heures
du matin on a pris les amures a tribord vent devant, dans la matinée on a
Distribuée, ou fixée les postes a Chaque hommes de l'équipage, pour le combat
et fait l'exercice du canon, a midi j'ai observée de latitude Sud . 29° 21;

19.° N.O.20; R.te des 24.h.res corrigé le S.O, 4¾ Sud, Chemin id .... 84. miles

longitude arrivé orientale meridien de paris .... 56.° 2;

Du 27. au 28. floréal

Pendant ce 24. heures. le tems a été beau, le vent variable du Sud a l'E.S.E
petit frais, presque Calme, on tenu le plus près durent, Sur differents bord
Suivant le vent, tenant la bordée qui, qui nous éllerait le plus au Sud, la mer
belle, toutes voiles dehors a midi j'ai observée de latitude Sud . 29° 41,

18.° N.O.20; R.te Courru Corrigé le S.S.O, 1¾ Sud, Chemin Cinglé .... 52. miles

longitude orientale meridien de paris .... 55.° 22,

Du 28. au 29 floréal

le tems fort beau, la mer belle, le vent Soufflant du S.E. variable variable a l'E.N.E,
petit frais. a 2.h du matin il s'ett fixée au Nord, fait route au S.¼ S.E, tout dehors
a midi j'ai observée de latitude Sud .... 31° 35;

19.° N.O.21. Route des 24. heures le S.E.¼ Sud 3¾ S. Chemin id 124 miles

longitude arrivé estimé Orientale M. de paris .... 57° 12.

Gustave Alaux ⚓

LEFT AND OPPOSITE PAGE
Illustrations by Gustave Alaux
in *Surcouf, privateer,* by
Jean de la Varende, 1946.

The French privateers do not
have the same dark yet splendid
reputation as the "sea dogs"
of Elizabeth I. They were not
without merit, however, as the
English found out to their cost,
since privateers such as Jean
Bart (1650–1702), René
Duguay-Trouin (1673–1736)
and Robert Surcouf
(1773–1827) had a special
predilection for capturing English
ships. Many French privateers
came from Saint-Malo (hence
its French nickname of "city of
privateers" – and the English
one of "hornets' nest"). By 1693
the English had had enough and
sent a time-bomb – comprising
a thirty-metre powder magazine
full of cannonballs – into the
port of Saint-Malo, but the
currents swept the device out
to sea. The locals enjoyed the
firework display, and the only
casualty was an unfortunate cat.

Pirate, Giuseppe Verdi, Daniel Defoe, Balzac with
Argow the Pirate, Eugène Sue with *Kernok the
Pirate*, John Meade Falkner with *Moonfleet* and J.
M. Barrie with his magical *Peter Pan*.

Countless other writers – and musicians and
painters – have raised the pirate to the level of the
fable: deadly and disconsolate, he represents the
fallen angel, the quintessential rebel, the explorer
of the abyss, the night prowler, the figure lurking
at the outposts of history, the dark intriguer.

Although the privateer has also inspired poets and
storytellers, he governs other, less obscure and
less remote dreams. He is as cunning as a fox and
as provident as a squirrel, and even more immoral
than his pirate cousin (who at least has one creed
only, even if it is an abominable one). The privateer has two faces: he tacks in and out of society,
between good and evil. He is not given to burning
the bridges that he crosses. He prefers his open
horizons to have a limit somewhere and he always
ends up coming back home. Drake left Plymouth
and for three years led a life of abandon with
unswerving commitment and lack of pity. Yet,
when he returned to London, his queen spared
him from the gallows, and even showered him
with honours and glory. He was appointed mayor
and vice-admiral – which did not prevent him,
once he tired of bowing and scraping, of frills and

lace handkerchiefs, from boarding his ship once again and resuming his wicked ways. He was a pirate in fits and starts, flitting from the forbidden to the legal, from citizen to outcast, from civilisation to chaos, from history to the murky borders of history. He may sometimes have exercised the profession of pirate, but it was always with a fixed-term contract.

The true pirate was a different breed altogether – tragic, pure and beyond redemption. He did not renege on his oaths as all his actions were irrevocable. He harboured neither regrets nor nostalgia.

He had no wish to reform society as he abhorred society, repudiated it and had taken leave of it for ever. He tolerated no rules other than the ones that he had bestowed upon himself, with the approval of the Devil.

A retired pirate is like a thirty-metre ant – a contradiction of nature! With only a few exceptions (Morgan and some other renegades), the pirate of the Caribbean or the Indian Ocean could not – even if he had amassed tons of gold – return to the pastures of his youth to count the hours of his twilight years by his grandfather clock. He had an heroic morality. He had no desire to relinquish his freedom, for it was his tunic of Nessus, his prison. It embraced him and killed him. This is the final paradox of the pirate: resolving to make freedom his motto, he is yet so closely imprisoned in this freedom that it takes on the form of a yoke from which he cannot escape. His freedom flies the flag of his death.

They applied the formulae that Georges Bataille would study so thoroughly three centuries later in his theories of spending and loss. Languid women came to life in taverns, in order to hasten the fulfilment of Bataille's excellent programme: in a few nights of orgies, all the booty was frittered away. Rather than ending up in the copper and steel chests so beloved of Stevenson and Hollywood, pirate gold tended to disappear in the finery of some highly unscrupulous women.

The authorities who controlled these haunts were indulgent towards such debauchery. For example, the French governor Isaac Le Vasseur – who had the advantage of being Calvinist and hating the Spanish – protected the entrances and shores of Tortuga by building a fort after he took it back from the Spanish. The Spanish succeeded, however, in reconquering the island, until Le Vasseur chased them out yet again a few years later in 1656. The governor tried to put Tortugan society to order, but old age had made him a crotchety authoritarian and he ended up being killed by his subordinates. Meanwhile, the Dutch were trading in the Caribbean, often illegally, from bases in the Gulf of Mexico (Campeche) or Honduras. They were

"It is evening on your island and round about, here and there, everywhere where the faultless vase of the sea swells out; it is the evening with the colour of eyelashes, on the woven paths of the sky and the sea.
Everything is salty, everything is viscous and heavy like the life of the plasmas.
The bird cradles itself in its feather, under an oily dream; the hollow fruit, deaf from insects, falls into the water of the creeks, digging its noise.
The island sleeps in the creek of the vast waters, washed with hot currents and fat roes, in the company of sumptuous silts."
Saint-John Perse,
Images to Crusoe.

OPPOSITE
Captain's head, illustration by
Gustave Alaux in *The Pig boucan*
by A. T'Sterstevens.

LEFT
In the tavern, illustration by
Gustave Alaux in *The Pig boucan*
by A. T'Sterstevens.

Protestants who hated Catholics; the memory of the Sea Beggars still exerted a fascination over them and they encouraged the raids of the free-booters. Moreover, the United Provinces were fighting the Spanish everywhere, be it in the Far East (the Sundan islands, Macao, India, etc.) or the Americas. Portugal and Holland were continually filching gulfs, promontories and trading posts from each other, as if playing blind man's buff. They chopped up the globe and shared out the bloody morsels. As far as Holland was concerned, anything that weakened the commercial or naval power of the Iberian countries was good news.

That is why the sailors of the United Provinces supplied the French and English freebooters of the Caribbean with arms and ammunition. They sometimes even lent them manpower. Some of their captains, such as the famous El Pirata who set himself up in the island of Curaçao, off the coast of Venezuela, in the early 1600s, took up banditry quite openly. El Pirata, whose real name was Cornelis Corneliszoon and who went by the nickname "Pie de Palo" or peg leg, was a man of

The fabulous booties used to evaporate in just a few nights: as soon as a successful expedition returned, the news spread all over Tortuga and on to Jamaica and Santo Domingo, and a horde of crooks and women converged on the taverns. What followed resembled a grotesque carnival. The lame and the one-eyed, the grimy and the hairy, the magnificent and the incomparable, clothed in rags of gold, muslin and silk, gave out handfuls of pieces of eight and silver ingots. They drank themselves into a stupor, guzzled themselves sick, caressed women and covered them with emeralds. And when the rum-induced haze was cleared, they were penniless. The pirate treasure was just a dream.

"On these occasions, my master bought a whole cask of wine, put it into the street and forced all the passers-by to drink with him, even threatening those who did not consent to do so. At other times, he did the same thing with barrels of beer or ale; often, with his own two hands, he threw these liquids into the street and sprayed the clothes of the pedestrians, without considering whether he was spoiling their costumes, or whether they were men or women."
Oexmelin.

remarkable cunning. In 1653 he dressed all his sailors as Franciscan friars and introduced himself at the entrance to Santiago de Cuba. The Spanish government received them attentively and hastily sent out a boat to welcome them. They shortly found themselves inside the city, and went on to pillage it. The word freebooter comes from the Dutch *vrÿbuiter*, which means "he who makes booty freely".

The Spanish were not happy. They wanted to pillage America on their own, in peace and quiet, without any outside help. Why should they share the loot with those scoundrels from the Caribbean, those French and English, who were often, to cap it all, Huguenots or Calvinists? They started changing their tactics: their galleons no longer sailed alone, but formed heavily armed convoys.

This innovation reaped rewards, but the freebooters were astute and learned how to adapt to the new circumstances. Instead of pursuing Spanish ships, they regrouped and constituted impressive fleets that launched raids into the hinterlands – these are known as the dry-land expeditions, which left traumatic scars on the populations of Central America. This was the home of cities brimming with the precious metals of Peru and Mexico. Vera Cruz, Maracaibo and Cartagena all suffered heavily from these attacks. Towards the end of the seventeenth century, the picture began to change a little as European countries became more vigilant and exerted increasingly stricter control over their zones of influence. In 1665 the freebooters pledged themselves to the crown of France. In Santo Domingo, a new governor, de Cussy, sent soldiers to attack the infamous bands. The pirate's life lost its charm: on this island, with the population of brigands decreasing from one thousand five hundred to a mere five hundred between 1681 and 1684.

It must also be pointed out that the system of alliances in Europe was in the process of being transformed. The disputes that were destroying the Old Continent began to lose some of their bitterness, much against the interests of the pirates. Although the latter had in effect heartily mocked history, countries and states, they nevertheless used the great political – and therefore religious – quarrels of the European capitals to ply their trade. They developed their project of escaping history under the protection of history – and they could

obviously perpetrate their atrocities more easily in a turbulent world than in a peaceful one.

They thrived in the cracks that ran through states. These cracks were now closing. The treaties of Utrecht, signed between 1713 and 1715, finally put an end to the brawl sparked by the succession of Spain, after the enthronement of Louis XIV's grandson, Philip V, in Madrid in 1700. The Utrecht agreements acknowledged Philip's right to the Spanish crown but, in exchange for recognising his empire, stripped him of his possessions in Italy and the Netherlands. France established its authority over its conquests. England con-

firmed its position as the ruler of the oceans, and Holland was too tired to pick any more fights with it. For the first time in ages, peace reigned over all lands and all seas, and this did not benefit the freebooters. The skimpy pretexts, whether patriotic or religious, with which these scoundrels had adorned their activities became threadbare and then disintegrated, one after another, along with the complicity granted them by kings at war. Order returned to Tortuga and, in part, to Santo Domingo, and the English pirates abandoned Jamaica. The good old days of the wild-pig hunters and freebooters had come to a close.

The dry-land expeditions

Any neat classification of the flotsam and jetsam of these accursed sailors is to be approached with caution. How is it possible to paint with the same brush such contrasting species, with so many genuses and varieties? How is it possible to group under the same heading the wild-pig hunters of Tortuga; the freebooters with their grapnels and sloops, their shrieks and grimaces; the "dry-land" adventurers, violent and destructive but as disciplined as any royal army; and the pirates who, a century later, basked in the paradises of the Indian Ocean, in order to nab the fabulous loot of the Great Mogul? It is far more satisfying to hop from island to island, from Tortuga to Madagascar, from Campeche to New Providence, picking out the most remarkable figures from this illustrious company of rogues.

In around 1635, Pierre le Grand left Dieppe in a rudimentary ship with twenty-eight sailors. Shortly after, he was to be found cruising in the Caribbean, off the shore of Hispaniola, where he came across a huge Spanish vessel. Pierre le Grand wanted to attack it, but his crew was fearful and had other ideas. Peter came up with a ruse: he ordered his surgeon to make some holes in the bottom of the ship and his freebooters, under threat of drowning, suddenly found hidden reserves of courage. They jumped on to the enemy deck and clambered up the stays, screaming all the while. The Spanish thought that they were banshees and did not find time to fire even one of their fifty-four canons. Pierre le Grand and his riff-raff found a veritable treasure in the hold. He considered himself to be rich and saw no point in making any further expeditions. He returned to France with his band and nothing more was heard of him again.

Most of Pierre le Grand's fellow pirates were less sensible. François (or Jean-David) Nau was known as the Olonnias, as he was born in the Sables-d'Olonne. He arrived in the Caribbean in 1650, at the age of twenty, and went on to enter Tortuga's hall of fame, thanks to his ferocity and ruthlessness. He hunted down Spanish ships in the sea round Cuba before inventing, with his friend Michel the Basque, the concept of "dry-land piracy". He seized towns at the head of a troop of four hundred ruffians. The pillage of Maracaibo in the Gulf of Venezuela, in 1666, was his doing – and it earned him three hundred and sixty thousand crowns.

This was a handsome profit, but freebooters had slippery fingers, and all these crowns slid through

Pirates were excellent navigators, even though their vessels had little in the way of maps, charts, astrolabes or astronomical crosses. They made up for this, however, with their flair and imagination. They used birds, clouds or the contours of a coastline to guide them, especially in the Caribbean. When pirates ventured into the vast expanses of the Atlantic or the Indian Ocean, they did require some instruments, or at least a compass and a telescope. An astronomical cross would give them some idea of their latitude, but there was no way to calculate longitude before the late 18th century. So, ships could tell roughly where they were in the north-south dimension, but were totally in the dark as regards their east-west position. Any maps that pirates acquired in the course of their pillaging were highly prized assets, as they could provide information of not only coastlines but also winds and sea routes and the position of ports, harbours, moorages, fortresses and citadels visited by enemy ships.

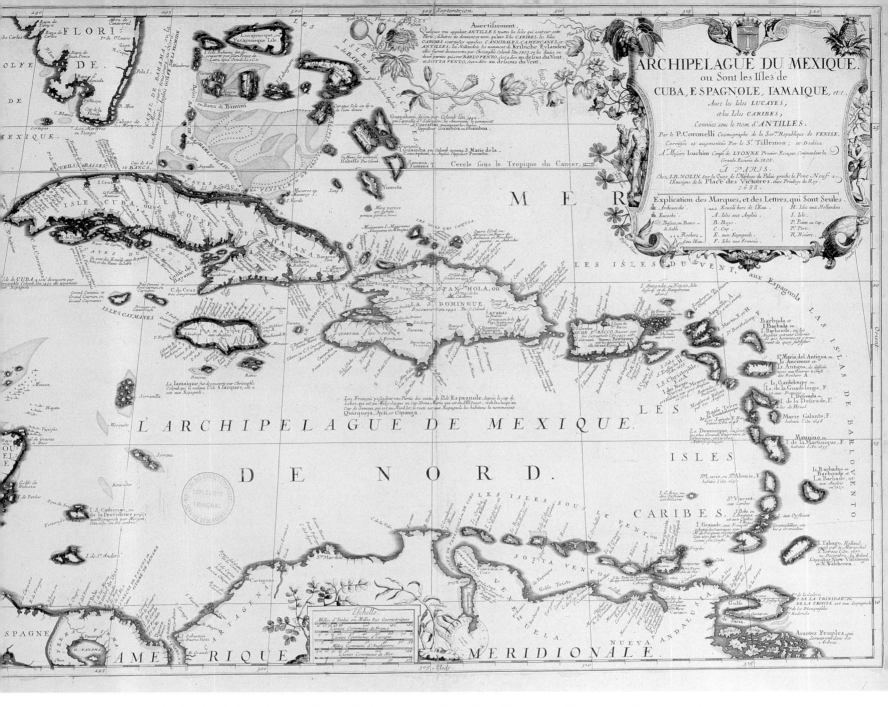

the hands of the Olonnais (although these were resplendent with gold and silver rings).

In desperate straits, he took to sea again, but then returned to dry land to sack Nicaragua and Honduras. Sometimes he set light to their towns, on other occasions he massacred all their inhabitants. One of his favourite games was cutting a prisoner's heart out in order to make another prisoner eat it.

The Olonnais, however, unlike most of the freebooters, was clumsy when it came to handling a ship. He got his yards mixed up and often ran aground. In 1671 his ship crashed into an islet inhabited by Bravo Indians, who cut him up, roasted him and then had him for dinner.

Rock Braziliano was a Dutchman who grew up in the Bahia region of Brazil. In 1654, the Portuguese chased out the Dutch, and Rock became separated from his parents, much to his distress. He would never forget that moment, and his subsequent career was motivated by a tireless and implacable desire for revenge against Iberian sailors.

He headed for the Caribbean. After some not particularly fruitful sojourns in Tortuga and Jamaica, he met the Olonnais and joined forces with him to capture a large prize. The two men had similar talents and understood each other to perfection. Rock matched the Frenchman's stern, imposing appearance – he had a curling moustache and hair parted down the middle – but his clothes were less

93

organised his life like a country squire. He had a sense of family and, in 1666, married the daughter of his uncle Edward, Mary Elizabeth Morgan. And when he pillaged a city, he was less prodigal than his men. He saved part of his booty to buy sugar plantations and slaves. He thought of the future and established a good relationship with the authorities on Jamaica. To be sure, like everybody else, he loved a good party with young women and rum but, in his early years at least, he held himself in check and put limits on his extravagances.

All that changed with old age, however. In 1667 the English and the Spanish decided to call a truce in the New World. Charles II, who had been restored to the throne in 1660 by General George Monk, was sympathetic towards Catholicism and encouraged tolerance. Unfortunately, the English governor of Jamaica, who was a friend of Morgan, took no notice of this agreement. To make his attitude crystal-clear, he commissioned Morgan to organise an expedition to Cuba. Morgan assembled ten ships and several hundred men. Three

hundred French freebooters from Tortuga signed on as well. Once in Cuba, Morgan had few problems in taking the city of Puerto Principe, but found little gold. His French allies were disappointed and abandoned the operation. Morgan continued towards Porto Bello, where all the gold from the coast of Panama was gathered together once a year. Porto Bello was a fiercely defended and heavily armed citadel, protected by three forts, and the freebooters were hesitant. Morgan summoned up their courage and, above all, instead of approaching from the sea, led his men via a roundabout route to the north. They attacked by land, through the inextricable jungle. The Spanish were amazed to see the freebooters spring out of the forest, instead of emerging from the sea. In the hue and cry that followed, the three forts of Porto Bello fell one by one.

Morgan demanded a fortune from Panama. The Spanish governor refused, much to Morgan's amusement. The Spanish counter-attacked, mobilising some of their best troops, but it took them several weeks to reach Porto Bello. During that time, Porto Bello was ruled by festivity and death. The freebooters killed, interrogated, tortured and ferreted out all the treasure in the city. After three weeks the Spanish warriors finally arrived in front of the forts, like a squad of ghosts, exhausted by their journey through the jungle. Morgan crushed them and returned to Jamaica with two hundred and fifty thousand pesos.

Spain was indignant and protested to the English court but Charles II, who dreaded a Spanish attack on Jamaica, resorted to frightening the Spanish by brandishing his magnificent freebooter. It should be added that, in Jamaica itself, Morgan was untouchable. He was considered a hero and, what is more, a hero with a touch of gold. Never before had the island been so prosperous. So, Morgan was able to prepare for his next battles undisturbed.

In 1668 he once again allied himself with the

Leur terrible, étendard à tête de mort au vent, ils débarquent en Nouvelle Biscaï.

Relation du Capitaine bordelais Massertie.

Tillac inv. et del.

French freebooters. The collaboration started off in boisterous good spirits, with the French and English sailors meeting on an island off Hispaniola to draw up their plans. They set their sights on Cartagena, in the Gulf of Darien (now in Colombia), whose port served as a staging post for Spanish ships on their way from Cadiz. To celebrate their pact, the French and English organised an orgy on board Morgan's ship. They drank, danced and made merry until a powder keg exploded. The ship went up in the air, along with two hundred men. Pieces of freebooters were scattered all over the reddened sea. The surviving sailors dived into the bloody waves and cut the hands off their dead colleagues, so that the gold rings that they had loved to flaunt would slide more easily off their fingers. Morgan's army, badly shaken by this disaster, abandoned its plans to attack Cartagena. It preferred to march on Maracaibo and ravage the surrounding area.

Morgan himself survived the accident and, undeterred, was eager for more action. The following year, he came up with his most ambitious scheme so far. Why not attack the city of Panama, on the Pacific coast of the isthmus, which was always crammed to the gunnels with gold from Peru or silver from Potosi?

Morgan's army was substantial – two thousand five hundred men and fifty boats – and so began

an epic journey. The crossing of the isthmus, whether on foot or by river, was deadly, and many men succumbed to diseases such as yellow fever and dysentery. They were thin and hungry when they finally reached Panama. Instead of launching an attack, they first massacred a herd of cows in the vicinity; they roasted them and spent the night celebrating.

The next morning, they unleashed a ferocious barrage that decimated the defenders of the city; the Indians, however, who were under the orders of the Spanish, counterattacked by releasing two thousand bullocks. The marauders fired into them and the animals went wild. In the ensuing chaos, Morgan's men took the opportunity to slip into the city, or rather the flames of the city. Everything was reduced to ashes but, amidst this desolation, Morgan found a pretty young Spanish girl whom he took away with him. The freebooters searched for gold ingots, but to no avail. This setback irritated them, so they set about pursuing Spaniards

The treasure chest

Pirates made their way to the Caribbean because the seas there were beautiful and the police incompetent — and because it lay on a trail that ended in gold. As Philip Gosse observed, "It did not take long for the fame of Tortuga to spread throughout the Caribbean, attracting hordes of adventurers of all kind who could not resist the temptation of attacking the Spanish because of the chances of rapid enrichment that this entailed. Such extremes of fortune have always attracted certain types of daredevils and the situation was very similar to that of California around 1849, or that of the 1897 gold rush in Klondike".

Nevertheless, although a pirate's eyes may have bulged at the thought of Spanish gold, he was no Scrooge or Shylock — in fact, he was the very opposite. Whereas Scrooge set about accumulating gold in order to multiply it, the freebooter acquired it to fritter it away, to destroy it and almost to abolish it.

When a pirate got his hands on treasure — after endangering his own life — he put his booty to absurd use. He treated it in two ways, both senseless and both resulting in a dispersion of the gold that turned it into nothing. Sometimes he spent it, squandering it at full speed, getting rid of it as if he feared being burnt or infected by it. A few orgiastic nights would be enough to transform the gold, via rum and women's flesh, into a memory.

On other occasions he would lock his gold in a large trunk fortified with locks and bolts and bury it in a secret place. No doubt he also scrawled a doodle on a scrap of paper to enable him to dig up his doubloons and piastres later on, but the most productive virtue of these scribbled maps was to fire the imagination of Stevenson in *Treasure Island*, and those of children captivated by all that is fearful and incomprehensible. Even though the stashes of Henry Morgan and Avery did in fact exist, it cannot be denied that the destiny of a pirate's gold, whether squandered or buried, was to serve for nothing. It existed as a mere fascination, an eclipsed sun, a hidden god. It was no more than a dazzling will-o'-the-wisp. Similarly intriguing are the nine pounds of gold that Arthur Rimbaud lugged round in his belt under the merciless sun of Abyssinia, at the risk of catching dysentery or even dying. It was another poet — one of the greatest, Yves Bonnefoy — who has best understood the avidity of Rimbaud.

"Symbolically", said Bonnefoy, "it is true that the kilos of gold that Rimbaud carried in his belt preserved the memory of a metaphysical sun once sought in vain,

and they caused a remnant of the irrational to gleam, beyond any rational project.
If my sickness resigns itself
If I ever have some gold,
Will I choose the North
Or the lands of the Vines?"
Christopher Columbus had already said, with respect to gold: "It is excellent.
Whoever owns it does everything he wants in this world and can even take souls
right up to Paradise".
Such debauched uses of this precious metal undoubtedly baffle chartered account-
ants and bankers, but they speak to all those children who have spent their nights
searching for the treasure that was also coveted by Long John Silver. "The word
treasure", wrote Roger Caillois, "silent and snuffed out for an adult, engages a
child with eloquent discourse and shines in his eyes with the most luminous
glow. Those syllables that age, experience and reflection soon render useless still
gleam like the riches they designate. They twinkle like the doubloons heaped up
by the pirates of old in dark caves, like the rubies, emeralds and so many other
sparkling stones that glimmer in the grubby hands bringing them out into the
light of day. It is not enough to say that children believe in treasure. They possess
it... Thus, in myths, powerful, barely conceivable objects are brought back from
the other world – golden apples, a blue bird, water that sings".
We already knew that the roaring of the freebooter's bombards are heard under
skies other than our own, on forbidden seas. The treasures of brigands and freebooters teach us the same lesson: the gold of pirates is not of this world.

17th-century sailor's trunk.

105

for a whole month. When they caught one, they treated him in their customary manner, and this usually led to them finding some gold or silver. Nevertheless, the pickings were modest and, to make matters worse, the booty had to be divided between many men, leaving little for each one.

The Frenchmen from Tortuga grumbled, suspecting that they were being swindled. Morgan's reply was to accuse them of hiding their prizes, and he ordered that they be searched. The French flew into a rage and the atmosphere became tense. Morgan was not a patient man and set sail, leaving his men behind. The story goes that he had kept a sizeable stash for himself and that he buried it in a secret place somewhere on his way back to Jamaica. Even today, treasure hunters comb jungles, beaches and islets in search of Morgan's treasure but of course they find nothing. Pirate gold is a philosophical gold.

The Spanish took umbrage and demanded that England forsake its freebooter. London played for time. This was a new version of the drama that had set England and Spain – Elizabeth I and Philip II – against each other a century before, over the

issue of another adventurer, Francis Drake. This time it was Charles II of Spain – a sickly individual whose seemingly imminent death was the subject of great speculation in all the courts of Europe – who was pitted against his namesake, Charles II of England.

Spain whiningly insisted that Morgan should be neutralised. At first the King of England prevaricated, just as Elizabeth I had done before him. Spain, however, piled on the pressure: was not Morgan responsible for violating the treaties signed by Madrid and London? The English king was driven into a corner and finally, in 1672, he ordered the arrest of Henry Morgan. The freebooter came back to London, but great care was taken not to imprison a free spirit of such ferocious magnitude, as that would only make his temper rise even more. Morgan went free and was feted wherever he went. Just like Drake a hundred years earlier, Morgan became the toast of London's salons.

Charles II turned a blind eye. Two years later, he decided to bestow a knighthood on Morgan. And, then, why not use Sir Henry's talents, experience, contacts and prestige to bring Jamaica to heel, now that it was overrun by disreputable brigands. Morgan changed his profession: the pirate became a hunter of pirates. He was appointed lieutenant general and dispatched back to Jamaica. He was, naturally, extremely good at his new job. He knew all the ins and outs of the freebooters' tactics and ruses. A former thief usually makes an excellent cop. (A good example is Vidocq – who appeared under the fictional name of Vautrin in several works by Balzac – in the early nineteenth century. He was a great sleuth precisely because he had previously been a great crook.)

Morgan proved highly enterprising in his new role – maybe a little too much so. The people of Jamaica objected when he set about pursuing his former comrades and bringing them to justice.

BELOW
Pirates transporting rum to exchange it for slaves, in *The pirate's own book*, 1837.

RIGHT
The Chevalier de Grammont, 1686, illustration by Debelle in *History of pirates and corsairs of the ocean and the Mediterranean, from their origin to the present* by P. Christian, 1846.

Grammont had a bad reputation. The Spanish considered his men "the Devil's butchers". Furthermore, he was insolent. When the governor of Hispaniola implored him not to launch a raid on Campeche by arguing that Louis XIV had forbidden it, Grammont retorted: "How could King Louis disapprove of a plan he knows nothing about and was only drawn up a few days ago?" One witness, however, presents a more pacific picture, praising "his grace, his generosity, his eloquence, his sense of justice".

Morgan claimed he could not care less, but his health began to fail him. He took to drink, spending more and more time in the dives of Port Royal. He was eventually brought to court on a charge of public drunkenness and stripped of his public functions. This Devil's song was not entirely played out, however. A few years later he was back in all his glory, but he could not keep up the rhythm. He was worn out, uncouth and as stubborn as a mule. He sent English doctors packing and put his trust in a local medicine man, but no sorcery could save him. Sir Henry Morgan died on 25 August 1688.

The French freebooters did not have the same panache but they nevertheless produced some strikingly sinister anti-heroes. Michel de Grammont, for example, came from a refined background but when, at the age of fourteen, he saw his sister flirting with a gentleman, he killed the hapless suitor. He then enlisted as a cabin boy on a ship bound for the Caribbean. As he was alert and well-schooled, he soon found himself being a commander, but obedience did not prove his

strong point. He liked the commanding part well enough, but serving the king had less appeal. He left the navy and acquired his own ship.

He became known as the General. He was indeed a soldier of the first order, although his atheism and outspokennness shocked even his fellow freebooters. He began cutting a swathe through Central America in 1672, shortly after Morgan. He sacked Maracaibo, Cumana and Veracruz, where he encouraged the local dignitaries to pay him a ransom by locking them in the cathedral and surrounding the building with powder kegs. This tactic earned him two hundred thousand crowns. In the following years, de Grammont experienced some setbacks. He asked for a pardon from the king of France and rejoined the Navy. He could not change his ways, however, and his repentance proved fleeting. Two years later, he set sail for Florida, but he was shipwrecked during the voyage – we do not know exactly where.

His band contained some remarkable figures, such as the Dutchman who went under the name of Van Horn, or sometimes Van Dorn. He was another talented sailor but somewhat prickly by nature. Although theoretically in the service of the king of France, he pursued his own, idiosyncratic interests. Whenever he saw a boat, for example, he would fire pot-shots at it, whatever

its flag. He formed part of de Grammont's army when it took Veracruz in 1682 but, in the excitement, got into an argument with another of de Grammont's sidekicks, Laurent de Graaf, also a Dutchman, who was famed for his courage and skill as a marksman. Van Horn was injured in the subsequent fight: his wounds became infected and he died. As for De Graaf, he gave up banditry and went on to help found New Orleans.

One of the last great freebooter expeditions took place in 1697, with Cartagena once again the unfortunate target. This foray was exceptional, however, in that it combined the forces of the freebooters with those of France itself. Louis XIV, who was caught up in the War of the League of Ausburg, was keen to get his hands on the rich city of Cartagena, whose harbour always contained ships full of gold from Peru. He entrusted the governor of Santo Domingo, Baron de Pointis, with this mission; he in turn enlisted several hundred freebooters to fight alongside the two thousand soldiers sent especially to the Caribbean, with the promise of a royal pardon for their past misdeeds. He had, however, naively failed to realise that freebooters were more interested in pillage than in fighting. In fact, they took little part in the battle but, once the city had fallen, they invaded its streets in search of gold.

The pirates of the Enlightenment

The eighteenth century may have seen the dawn of the Enlightenment, but any enlightenment by the successors of the freebooters in the waters of the Americas, the Atlantic and the Indian Ocean was distinctly murky, shedding more darkness than brightness.

It is, however, impossible to ignore the strange parallels between the strivings of the major European nations and those of the pirate captains. Just as voyagers of the Enlightenment, from Bougainville to Captain Cook and La Pérouse, intended to put the entire planet under the protection of their masters and laws, pirates sought to extend to hitherto undifferentiated lands the utopia of pirate society, the desire for a world "without masters and laws".

This latest chapter in the pirate fable starts in the British colonies in North America, after the decline and extinction of the freebooters at the end of the seventeenth century. Philippe Jacquin, a historian of piracy and the New World, estimates that some five thousand Anglo-American pirates were wreaking havoc in these colonies between 1716 and 1726. The island of New Providence in the Bahamas took pride of place as one of the headquarters of large-scale piracy.

It was not difficult to find willing recruits among mutinous sailors as life onboard the ships of a king – be it that of England or France – was mercilessly harsh. The poorly paid sailors were despised, humiliated and ill-treated by their cap-

tains. They were tired of going hungry, of being punished for a triviality, of being lashed or almost asphyxiated when they were dragged along the length of their ship's keel on the end of a rope. They escaped at the first opportunity, and often put their courage and skill at the disposal of a pirate. As the century advanced, however, piracy in the Caribbean and the Americas faltered. Many pirates tried to recycle themselves by searching for new waters and new challenges.

Some prowled the coasts of Sierra Leone or Dahomey and tried their hand at the slave trade, buying Africans and then delivering them to the Americans of Virginia, New York and Charleston. At the same time, long-distance piracy on the high seas began to flourish. Just as English nobles invented the concept of an investigative journey that served as a rite of passage into the mysteries of art, the pirates of the Enlightenment perfected a somewhat different kind of initiation, which focussed less on the works of Leonardo da Vinci or Italian cathedrals and more on the gold, precious stones and silks of the East Indies. This piratical rite of passage started in North America, continued round the Cape of Good Hope and went on to the Indian Ocean, the Red Sea, the Persian Gulf and the Malabar Coast.

Space does not permit us to examine all these pirate populations; besides, many are lost in history, never to be recovered. We can, however, put them into a few broad categories.

ABOVE
Attack by freebooters in
The Pig boucan,
by A. T'Sterstevens.
Illustration by Gustave Alaux.

When the freebooters faded away in the 1720s, pirates changed their playgrounds. They left Tortuga and Hispaniola to infest the Bahamas, particularly the area around New Providence (now Nassau). They attacked the ships that supplied the British colonies in the Americas. The governor of South Carolina described them as a "calamity for the poor province". Resistance to piracy became more organised, forcing the marauders to set their sights further afield. They crossed the Atlantic, launching raids in Africa and spreading to the Comoros Islands and Madagascar. Not that we can talk about a piracy "route" – pirate boats were always drunken ones.

RIGHT
Illustration by Louis Marque for "The Gold-Bug",
by Edgar Allan Poe.

113

Why our slave? by Jean-Baptiste Carpeaux.

Pirates made forays into the slave trade. Back in the 16th century, one of Elizabeth I's seadogs, the "very good and very gallant knight Sir John Hawkins", had set the example: he used to catch Africans in the Gulf of Guinea. Two centuries later, when piracy made inroads into the Atlantic and the Indian Ocean, many a pirate ship dabbled in the slave trade at one time or another. Black people were also well represented in the crews of pirate ships, just as they would be among the American cowboys. One third of the sailors on Bartholomew Roberts' ships were black.

Opposite
The disembarkation of Negroes in James Town, 1619. Illustration for *Colonies and Nations* by Woodrow Wilson by Howard Pyle, 1901.

There follows an attempt to put this rogues' gallery in order: in top rank, the *Devil's disciples*, who were mainly found in the Americas; then, the *drifters*, who were scattered everywhere; next, the *scallywags*, who revelled in the good life of the Indian Ocean; and, finally, the *pirates under the banner of good*.

THE DEVIL'S DISCIPLES

The Englishman Edward Low was a cold-hearted monster. After a brief period working in the docks of Boston, he stole a boat, teamed up with some other ne'er-do-wells and headed for the coast of Honduras. In 1722 and 1723 he got up to no good in the Caribbean, as well as off the coasts of America and Newfoundland. Low was an extremely vindictive man who bore a grudge against both the Spanish and the sailors of New England, and these grudges kept him fully occupied. When he cornered an enemy he was beside himself with joy, licking his licks in anticipation. His smile was enough to terrify his prisoners. Sometimes he sliced open their throats personally with a huge cutlass; on other occasions, he made them run on the deck and invited his crew to lunge at them with their knives, so that the poor unfortunates were hacked to death. When he was bored, he looked for ways of killing time. One day he had the idea of cutting the lips off one of his captives and cooking them. Low did have a sensitive side, however, and was even given to crying when he contemplated his death. Not that he was afraid of the gallows; he was not concerned about dangling at the end of a rope, it was just that his son would suddenly be orphaned when it happened.

Low's crew became so sick of his barbarity that they decided to cast him off in a rowing boat – having first taken the precaution of removing the oars. Fortunately, Low was spotted by a ship and rescued; unfortunately, the ship was French and it took him to Guadeloupe, where he was hanged – although his

legend refused to die so soon, and seemingly reliable witnesses swore that they had sighted him in the Caribbean long after his execution.

Captain Fly operated on the coasts of Guinea and North America. His favourite expression was: "God damn you!" He was finally hanged in Boston. His tarred body was then put on public display in the port.

Captain Lewis was an abject specimen who seemed to have come straight from Hell. While still a boy he appeared one day, slightly supernaturally, on the deck of a ship commanded by one Captain Bannister, and nobody could work out how he had got onboard. As he was extremely agitated, he was hung by the middle of his body from

117

the mizzenmast. This treatment had the desired effect and the boy calmed down.

Later on, Lewis became a ship's captain. His links with Satan were undeniable, and they imbued him with vanity, glory and a melancholy streak. He spoke a string of languages, which was usually a speciality of the Holy Spirit, but was not Satan a fallen angel? Did this linguistic gift, bestowed on a man so brazenly perverse, confirm the fact that extreme wickedness and extreme kindness are equally polyglot?

Lewis told his subordinates that somebody came to visit him onboard from time to time, and that that somebody was Satan. On these occasions, Lewis had a military briefing from Satan, who gave out orders, elaborated projects, traced routes and offered strategic advice. One day, Captain Lewis announced that Satan had indicated the time of his forthcoming death – and he did in fact die at exactly that time.

Edward Teach – Blackbeard – was the most famous of the New Providence pirates. He has been fêted by the cinema and literature and inspired dozens of paintings – even giving rise to a few veritable masterpieces – but his period of most intense activity, on the coasts of America and the Caribbean, was extremely short, no more than eighteen months.

The extent of Blackbeard's legacy to literature is not really surprising, as he had an acute sense of

dramatic staging. He was a fine sailor with an awe-inspiring presence. His contemporaries, particularly Daniel Defoe, in his extensive history of piracy, described him, yet again, as a comrade of the Devil.

Teach, born in England in 1680, first operated as a privateer, but very soon decided that it was better to work for himself. Setting off for the coasts of Virginia and the Carolinas, he attacked the port of Charleston. He took a city councillor's son – barely four years old – as hostage and did not release him until he received a trunk full of medicines. He pillaged some boats but often got into arguments with his crew, who resented his brutal behaviour. Once, after a quarrel, he abandoned most of his crew on a sand bank in the Bay of Honduras and headed for Bath, North Carolina, where he was warmly welcomed. He bought a house in Ocracoke, one of the islands off the Outer Bank that protects North Carolina from the whims of the sea. He married a rich young woman but there was little improvement in his character. In 1718, he organised the biggest reunion of pirates ever witnessed – and the biggest orgy.

The governor of Virginia was infuriated by this scoundrel. He sent two Royal Navy ships to Ocracoke, under the command of one Captain Maynard. Blackbeard and his men stormed onboard the enemy vessels and there followed a

fight to the death between the two leaders. Blackbeard, who was amazingly strong, gained the upper hand but, when he was about to go in for the kill, one of Maynard's sailors struck him on the neck. Blackbeard bled profusely but he had nine lives (as people would later remark about Rasputin). He carried on fighting, but Maynard's men gathered round vociferously to support their captain. Blackbeard lost more and more blood before finally collapsing and dying. Maynard, who was distrustful by nature, cut off his head to be on the safe side and attached this splendid trophy to the prow of his ship.

In his old hunting grounds, Blackbeard had become a legend. Some ten names were attributed to him – Drummond, Tash, Thatch, etc – as well as fourteen different wives. His strategies and tactics were the subject of hot debate. Innkeepers, retired pirates and maybe even the grandmothers of Port Royal, Charleston and Ocracoke regaled listeners with accounts of his exploits.

When Blackbeard launched an attack, he made himself appear horrific in order to strike fear into the hearts of his enemy. Hemp wicks coated with saltpetre were attached to his hat and when they were lit his ugly faced grimaced in a cloud of smoke. What is more, he belched profusely, making a dreadful noise. Six pistols hung from his belt. He used his long musket as a bludgeon, and a single blow was enough to kill a man outright.

DRIFTERS

Why did somebody become a freebooter, a pirate or a sea beggar? Some of them were swept along by a fateful destiny. For example, they were passionate about the sea, or they were attracted by the excitement of crime; when these two enthusiasms merged, the result was larger-than-life diabolical figures like Lewis and Low. Others, however, became pirates by chance, through lack of attention or by surprise. They were "ordinary men", or drifters whom we would nowadays call antiheroes. In their youth, they seemed reasonable and passed unnoticed but, one day, they made a mistake or argued with their master or rashly bought a boat and had to find something to do as they had spent their last penny on the vessel – so they called themselves a "pirate" and a few years later sailed off into the distance.

There are cases like this throughout the history of piracy. One of the scourges of the Elizabethan period, the Frenchman Francis Verney (1584–1615), had a wife with a harsh character who did not obey him at all. When he could stand her no longer, he went to the port, sailed away on a ship and killed any Englishmen who crossed his path. He ended up in Algiers, disguised as a Turk. with a long purple tunic trimmed with fur and gold topped off by a heavily embroidered head-dress. He was eventually captured by an Italian galleon, however, and condemned to hard labour. He was unable to endure this indignity for long and died at the age of thirty-one.

Another Frenchman, Montbars, was a young man from a good family but, when a schoolteacher informed him that the Spanish mistreated American Indians, he became so indignant that he set sail for the Caribbean. There, he gleefully sunk so many Spanish ships that he earned the nickname "Exterminator".

The Welshman Bartholomew Roberts (1682– 1722) became a pirate by chance. He was sailing without thinking of anything particular when his boat fell into the hands of a brigand. This struck him as being an interesting trade so he started calling himself Black Bart and joined the profession himself, soon displaying great talent. It is said that he captured around four hundred ships.

Stede Bonnet, sometimes known as William Bonnet, was a wealthy scion of the middle-class, well educated and much admired. His life on a huge plantation in Barbados was indolent and his nights were untroubled. It is easy to imagine him

sitting in his rocking chair and gazing at the gleaming backs of the slaves toiling away in his cane fields.

This idyll, however, was marred by his disagreeable wife. The pacific Stede Bonnet grew tired of the endless rows and decided to leave her. As he was rich, he bought himself a ship, along with ten cannons; he christened it *Revenge*, signed up seventy sailors and attacked a few boats off Virginia and North Carolina. His business was thriving but one day he ran into the fearsome Blackbeard. Bonnet was out of his class, and Blackbeard took his ship. This indiscretion enraged Stede Bonnet, who swore revenge and that he would kill

LEFT
Fleet Street: the Virginia planter's trade sign

RIGHT
Captain Avery attacking a ship of the Great Mogul.

Mr. Bonnet was a businessman in the Caribbean. Prosperous and reasonable, although somewhat melancholy. Watching the bustle in the port suddenly instilled in him the desire to leave. He became a pirate. Just like that, without any warning. He abandoned everything and became an outlaw. He was still prosperous but, ultimately, unreasonable. The melancholy returned, however. He went back to the port. He was pardoned, put away his earring and headscarf and took on a respectable life once again. Besides, there were hardly any pirates left. They had all sworn their allegiance to the king, who offered them a pardon if they gave up freebooting. Or almost all of them. People greeted Mr. Bonnet in the street, just like old times, all the while whispering that he had had a kind of attack of imagination, but that it was over now, what a story, indeed, was he not a little bit French?

William Bonnet had a scar on his cheek. The ladies found him attractive. And then one day he went back to sea. He knew there was a noose at the end of it all. He went back to sea.

William Bonnet, the gentleman from the Caribbean.

And he died in the course of an attack.

Évelyne Pieiller

LEFT
Montbars the Exterminator, illustration by Lemaistre for *The fiancée of the white vulture*, by A. de Lamotte, *Veillée des Chaumières*, 12 February 1885.

RIGHT
The ravagers of the sea, Jules Ferrat, print, 1889.

Blackbeard. Meanwhile he went back to work and resumed his pillaging, this time under the name of "Captain Thomas". After a few years, however, Bonnet became bored and resolved to return to the straight and narrow. His destiny ruled otherwise, however. He came into the line of sight of two ships off Charleston; in a hail of cannonballs, he and his crew surrendered. He had passed the point of no return and, in November 1718, Stede Bonnet and twenty-nine sailors were hanged.

THE SCALLYWAGS OF THE INDIAN OCEAN

Two other pirates made their name in the Indian Ocean: Captain John Avery, also known as Long Ben, and Captain William Kidd. These two men had much in common: they were born in Britain, began their seafaring career hunting French pirates, would betray anybody and they without glory. Together they provide a good illustration of the splendour and decline of the pirates of the Indian Ocean.

William Kidd was born in the middle of the 17th century, into a middle-class family in Greenock,

Scotland. He enrolled in the Royal Navy, went to New York and married an heiress. At the age of forty, he obtained letters of marque that endowed him with the right – and duty – to attack every French ship he set his eyes on. He had no little success in the Caribbean, but was so severe with his subordinates that they mutinied. A few years later, the Caribbean was free of French pirates, so Kidd got himself a job: the Governor of New York commissioned him to capture as many freebooter ships as he could. Kidd headed for the Indian Ocean to purge the Red Sea of its riffraff.

Captain Kidd proved yet again that he was not a leader of men but rather a cowardly, hypocritical brute. His crew rebelled, questioning his orders. The ship was in uproar. Kidd was insulted by his chief gunner, and replied by observing that the gunner was "a verminous dog". The gunner did not dispute this zoological classification, but he did point out: "It's you that has made me like this". Kidd picked up a bucket with metal hoops and smashed it down on the gunner's head, killing him. This death was not without significance. It marked Kidd's passage from the condition of privateer to one of pirate. He no longer took any notice of the commission that the Governor of New York had signed for him. He attacked each and every ship that came within his range. In 1698, he won a particularly large prize: an Armenian ship, which he stripped of its merchandise. This escapade shocked the American authorities and, when Kidd arrived back in New York, he was promptly thrown in jail, before being shipped back to London to face trial at the Old Bailey.

Just a few sessions in court were sufficient to condemn him to death. The sentence was carried out on 23 May 1701 in Execution Dock, with his tarred body being displayed in an iron cage at Tilbury as a warning to other miscreants. He had a secret stash of booty and took its hiding place to the grave; Kidd's treasure has never been found.

126

A Prize

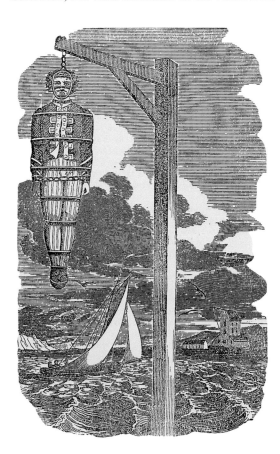

John Avery, or Long Ben, was an equally worthless specimen. He was born around 1675, in Plymouth. Like Kidd, he started out in merchant ships, but in the service of Spain. He embarked on the *Duke* to pursue French pirates in the Caribbean, but took command of the vessel after leading a mutiny. He then set off for Madagascar. Patrolling the Red Sea with a convoy of two sloops, he nabbed a magnificent catch: one of the ships of the Great Mogul. He found precious gems, 100,000 piastres and the Mogul's daughter. Avery lustily manhandled all the booty, especially the girl, who was very beautiful. As he was not given to sharing, he promised his associates that he would give them their portion at another time, in another place. He returned to the Caribbean and then to England to dispose of his spoils.

Avery was, however, preceded by his infamous exploits and treachery. English merchants were distrustful of him; they also knew that it would be hard to find a buyer for gems stolen from the Great Mogul. They offered him peanuts, but Avery was desperate and accepted.

How he enjoyed, for years, the status of "the king of pirates" – yet another one! – is a mystery. It was rumoured that he had married the daughter of the Great Mogul and was the king of Madagascar but it is now clear that he was a nobody and that, if he was a king, he was a "beggar king". By the time of his death, the general view was that he was not even worth the sum required to buy his coffin.

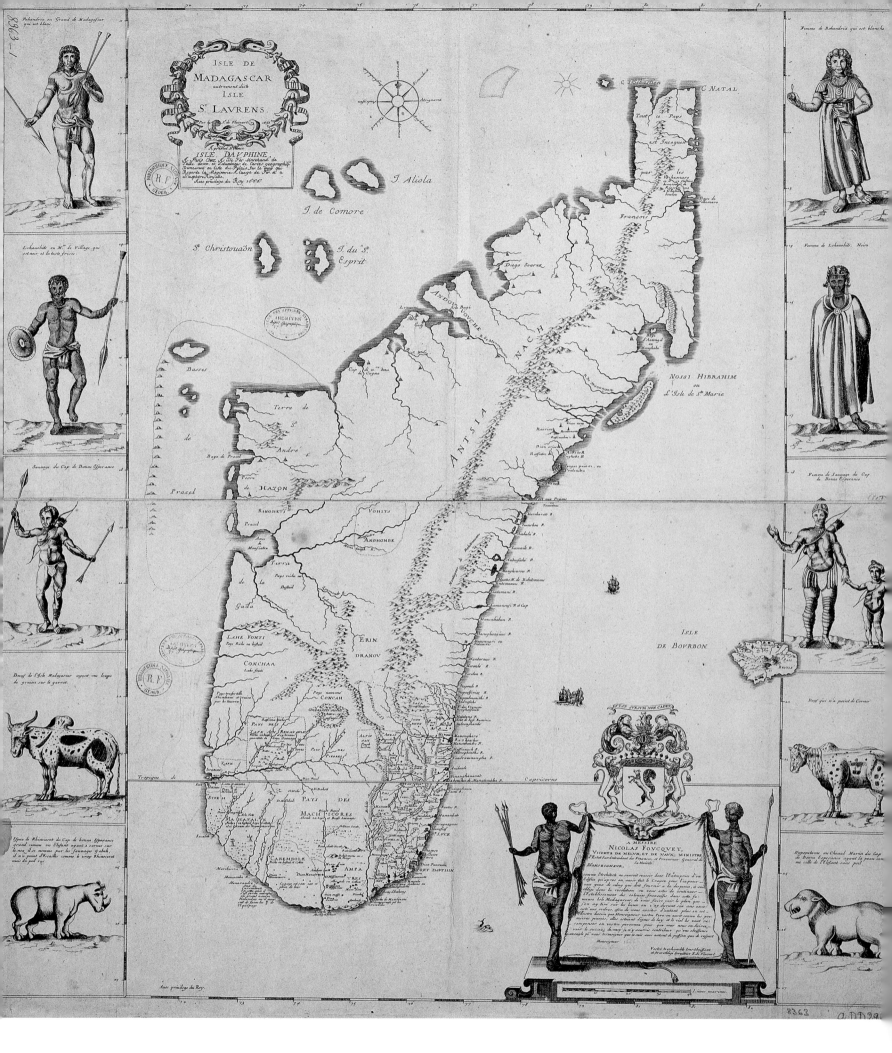

Pirates under the banner of good

Despite the black flag with the skull and cross-bones, despite the trail of blood, not all pirates were wicked. Some, of a more philosophical bent, tried to steer this industry of evil towards the territories of good.

These sensitive rascals could be found at the end of the 17th century and the start of the 18th century, generally in Madagascar and the Indian Ocean (maybe because of the languor of these climes).

The most famous of the followers of good was the Frenchman Captain Misson, who built a utopian city in the Bay of Diego-Suarez, in the late 17th century. He chose a perfect spot. When the Creator constructed this setting, He must have been remembering the descriptions of Eden in the Bible; lagoons and rustling palm trees, the scent of vanilla wafting through the night air, a sea gleaming like the sun and unchanging skies – the world of Hesodius. There, in the golden light of Claude Lorrain or Virgil, well-mannered pirates grew cassava and loved each other.

In the age of Louis XIV – so bitter and implacable towards the less fortunate – it could appear that all the good things in life had found a haven in Captain Misson's unlikely colony. Misson was born into a wealthy Protestant family in Provence; he was a brilliant student, with a special gift for logic, rational thinking and mathematics. As he also loved the sea, he enlisted on one of the King's ships, the *Victoire*.

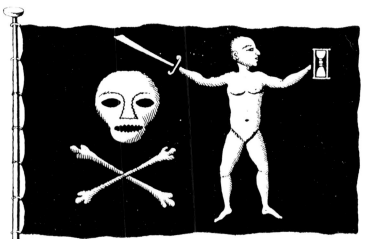

Pavillon de Ras de St Maur long de 22 pieds 9 pouces & large de 14 pieds 9 pouces

The ship stopped off in Italy, and in Rome Misson met one Carracioli, a garrulous, defrocked Dominican monk, who considered that the world was upside-down and governed by wickedness. Carracioli resisted this state of affairs, inspired by the vision of a merciful society. He loved only freedom and was set on remaking both the world and men. He remade God, Genesis, the Garden of Eden – he remade everything. Grasping the nettle, he was going to put the world to rights. He had an ideal: a project for a just and tolerant community that welcomed all races. His ideas, influenced by Joachim de Flore and anticipating Rousseau, Marx and Babeuf, astonished Misson. A friendship was forged between the two men, and Carracioli embarked on the *Victoire*.

Before long, the *Victoire* was sailing in the Caribbean, where it was attacked by an English ship. A brutal battle ensued, and all the officers onboard the *Victoire* were killed, except for

LEFT
Madagascar, formerly known as Saint-Laurent Island. Map by the Master of Flacour, 1656.

"They all worked at their tasks in peace, in the midst of prosperity. Rich in livestock, and beloved of the happy gods." Hesiodus, *The works and the days*.

HISTORIE DER ZEE-ROOVERS

Misson. Carracioli preached to anybody who would listen to him, and succeeded in persuading Misson and the crew to abandon the service of the king and declare themselves pirates. Misson needed convincing but the crew, imagining tons of gold, rum and women, were delighted.

No sooner said than done. The sailors were quickly disappointed, however. Their dreams were far from being fulfilled, and they saw that a pirate's life was no joyride in the company of these two bizarre characters; onboard the *Victoire*, which had changed course and was now heading first to Africa and then to the Indian Ocean, the slightest incident provided a cue for a sermon or a humanistic discourse.

Misson insisted that, if they were going to be pirates, then they would be pirates of virtue. Instead of the black flag of renegade sailors, the *Victoire's* would be an immaculate white and it would bear not a skull and crossbones but the

inscription "God and Liberty". This is what is known in philosophy as an "epistemological leap" and, true to form, it inspired a fine speech: "As we are not going to act in the manner of pirates, whose life and principles are dissolute, we must spurn their colours. Our cause is just, good, innocent and noble; it is the cause of Liberty. I am therefore of the opinion that we should adopt a flag with the figure of Liberty and, if you want a motto, *A Deo a libertate*, for God and Liberty, so that it will be the emblem of your uprightness and your resolution".

Once the *Victoire* had rounded the Cape of Good Hope, it went up the Mozambique Channel and docked in Anjouan, in the Comoros. Here, Misson married the sister of the Queen of Anjouan and sunk a Portuguese ship full of gold powder. He then borrowed a ship called *Bijou* from the Queen of Anjouan, which took the entire band to the Bay of Diego-Suarez.

Misson put down roots in Diego-Suarez, building cabins. The colony was christened "Libertalia". Rules were drawn up, and this bunch of rogues became paragons of virtue. Politeness and civility were no joking matter in Carracioli and Misson's brave new world.

On one stopover, for example, Misson unthinkingly took on some rather coarse Dutch sailors. Their vocabulary was peppered with curses and swearwords. Misson was afraid that immorality would creep into his enterprise by means of this foul language. He gave the Dutchmen some soap and explained that it was very dangerous to soil, by using vulgarity, the language that God had bestowed on men, because there was a danger of obscuring the "sole faculty that distinguishes man from beast: Reason". The Dutchmen were impressed and did not curse or swear any more. Just too make sure, Misson warned them that any recidivism would be punished with a beating.

LEFT
Frontispiece of a Dutch edition of Captain Johnson's book, with depictions of Mary Read and Ann Bonny.

"A long time ago, in the time of our forefathers, as the writings of the Ancients bear witness, people loved each other with a sensitive and loyal love, not out of covetousness or the desire for plunder, and good reigned over the world. The land had not yet been cultivated, but was as God had made it, and it alone provided everybody's means of subsistence."
Jean de Meung, *Roman de la rose.*

RIGHT
Nature is good and moderating. Mosaic in the Convent of San Francisco de Bahia, Salvador de Bahia, Brazil.

132

Heaven and Hell

Pirates had a religious sense. They defied both gods and men. They poured insults on priests, to be sure, but these imprecations were confessions.

They did not succeed in washing from their skin the stigmata of their baptism. The very virulence of their blasphemy was proof that they had failed to break out of the circle of their childhood and education, whether that circle was enchanted or terrible. The most diabolical pirates were the most perceptive witnesses of this struggle against a God who refused to let them go. Fly reproached one of his prisoners who was whimpering in the face of death, saying: "God damn him, but as he is so ridiculously sanctimonious, we shall give him the time to say his prayers, and I shall be the priest." Fly mumbled a prayer before slaughtering his prey.

One of Bartholomew Roberts' sailors, a certain Sutton, was about to be hanged with some of his colleagues. He noticed that one of his companions in evil was sobbing and praying fervently. He was intrigued:

"What do you hope to gain with your prayers?"

"Heaven."

"Heaven, are you mad? Have you ever heard of a pirate entering Heaven? I want to be in Hell. You are much better off there, and as soon as I arrive, I shall greet Roberts with thirteen blows."

Another of Roberts' sailors also bequeathed his philosophy:

"We despise the King, his Parliament and his pardon. We have even less fear of the gallows. If we are conquered or surprised, we shall set fire to the gunpowder and we shall go merrily to Hell, and in good company too."

These affronts to God and this respect for the Devil affirm that the pirate was a religious man. He may well have been immoral and sometimes repugnant, but he sailed in the waters of the sacred.

By joining up with such loathsome company, he chose to rub out the city, society, the century that witnessed his birth, the laws of his king — everything that was the work of men and time, the immanent, the ephemeral and the illusory; in short, the profane. In fact, and as if to confirm, or rather decode, the blasphemous fury of some captains, there are also numerous examples of superstition and devotion in freebooter crews.

Captain Daniel, who terrorised the Caribbean in the 17th century, cast anchor not far from Guadeloupe. There he found a priest. Daniel thanked the heavens. He would take the opportunity to purge his soul, which was a little sullied, and those of his sailors, which were hardly in any better state.

The priest was hoisted onboard. An altar was improvised on the poop deck. The holy sacrifice of the Mass began and, to show their appreciation, the sailors fired a few shots towards the heavens. The Elevation of the Host, however, was greeted in silence, although this was soon broken by an explosion and a scream. The priest shuddered. A sailor lay dead on the deck but Daniel, who was holding a smoking gun, shrugged this off: "Don't you worry, Father, he was a rogue who failed in his duties and I punished him so that he would learn to do better." Père Labat, who recounted this incident, cheerfully concluded: "That was an effective way of preventing him from repeating his errors."

Priests were few and far between in the pirate communities. If need be, their services could be dispensed with, but this scarcity meant that there was often a shortage of Bibles and holy scriptures. This was highly inconvenient for captains because every sailor was obliged, in principle, to swear on the Bible when he accepted the rules of a ship.

One day, a certain Captain Philips realised that his vessel's only Bible was missing. Another sacred object was sought. One sailor suggested using an axe; Philips thought this was an excellent idea, and from then on his recruits swore fidelity on the blade of an axe. Another pirate, De Soto, worked off the coasts of Africa in the early 19th century. He was bloodthirsty but refined; he ended up being caught in Gibraltar, and one eye witness described his death as follows:

"I think I have never seen anybody show a contrition equal to that manifested by this man. He did not show the slightest fear, however. He walked with a steady step behind the fatal cart, alternating his gaze from his coffin to the cross he held in his hand. He pressed the symbol of divinity firmly against his lips, repeated the prayers that the priest accompanying him whispered in his ear and seemed only to be concerned about the future world. When the procession reached the gallows, by the water's edge, the pirate got on the cart but, finding the rope too short, he jumped on his coffin and put his head in the dangling noose. Then, when he felt the cart shaking, he cried out "Adiós a todos", "Goodbye, everybody", and slumped forward."

Such examples are infinite, but the conclusion is always the same. Whether He is cursed or praised, God — the God of Christians, as it happens — is one of the main players in the pirate adventure. These gentlemen of fortune failed to shake Him off. They adored Him or detested Him, but they could not escape from Him. As Arthur Rimbaud wrote in *A Season in Hell*: "I am a slave to my baptism. Parents, you have made my wretchedness and you have made your own. Poor innocent! Hell cannot attack pagans."

Misson implemented a constitution with a socialist inspiration. All the inhabitants of Libertalia were free and equal under the law – just as French citizens would be a little later, after the storming of the Bastille. Power was exercised by elected councillors – with one councillor for every ten pirates – and a supreme leader or "conservative", who was Misson himself.

Daily life was strictly regulated. Money was kept in a communal kitty. It was forbidden to mark off any plot of land with a wall or a hedge. Misson was also innovative in another field; in a century in which some people were still asking whether black people had a soul, he provided an answer: Yes, they did – and so did Redskins and Asians. As a result, there was no racism in Libertalia. In the refectory, the custom was to alternate skin colours, as in a Benetton advert: one red, one white, one black and one yellow.

There was further sacrilege: Misson and Carracioli believed that the dispersion of languages was an effect of original sin. Therefore, if sin was to be rejected, it was prudent to join languages together. They set about congregating them all so that humanity could recover a single dictionary and thereby ultimately regain Paradise. Turning their backs on the false premise of the Tower of Babel, the pirates of Diego-Suarez invented a forerunner of Esperanto.

Like all utopias, like all "cities of glass", Libertalia ran into a stumbling block: in this case, it was sex. In his initial rush of excitement, Misson, avid for purity, imposed strict chastity on his subjects. This did not work very well, however, so Misson did an

FREE NATIVES OF DOMINICA.

This Plate is Dedicated to   *Sir W.ᵐ Young, Bar.ᵗ*

by his most Obliged and   *devoted Serv.ᵗ A. Brunias.*

London, Pub.d as the Act directs Feb.y 1, 1780,   by the Proprietor N.º Broad Street, Soho.

A. Brunias, pinx.t et sculp.t

about-turn: he replaced chastity with polygamy. This worked somewhat better. In this respect, Louis XIV's sailor was very faithful to general utopian trends. It is not uncommon that these "ideal cities", like the gnostic doctrines of old, veered between obligatory chastity and encouraged orgies.

The brotherly republic of Diego-Suarez operated for a few years, with anything up to 400 inhabitants. Its final days were sad, however, as they illustrate how goodness is not always understood even by those it seeks to embrace: the anti-racist city of Captain Misson was decimated by hordes of the natives that it sought to respect. The theorist behind the experiment, Carracioli, was killed, but Misson escaped and fled with two sloops and some fellow-citizens of Libertalia. He headed back for France, but never made it, as his ship was sunk en route.

Libertalia has inspired writers, musicians, filmmakers and historians. The French novelist, J. M. G. Le Clézio, who spent his childhood in Mauritius and loves maritime adventure stories, wrote in *The Prospector*: "I used to read books that spoke about pirates, and their names resonated in my imagination. The one I liked most was Misson, the pirate-philosopher who, with the help of the defrocked monk Carracioli, had founded the Republic of Libertalia in Diego-Suarez, where all men lived free and equal, whatever their origins and race."

Le Clézio's enthusiasm is easy to understand, but unfortunately Misson probably never existed. For a long time, nobody doubted the veracity of his adventure, and even respected scholars like Hubert Deschamps vouched for it. In the last few years, however, historians have changed Misson's classification and assigned him to the realm of legend.

The curious story of Libertalia was recounted by Captain Johnson in *A general history of the robberies and murders of the most notorious pirates*. This book, along with the more partial eye-witness accounts of Père Labat and Oexmelin, the freebooters' surgeon, constitutes the basis of our knowledge of pirates.

Who was this elusive Captain Johnson, so precisely informed about the tiniest details of pirates' lives? In 1939, a British academic, John Robert Moore, suggested in his essay *Defoe in the pillory*, that Captain Johnson was really Daniel Defoe (1658–1731), the author of *Robinson Crusoe and Moll Flanders*. The historian Hubert Deschamps was unconvinced and presented arguments to show that Defoe could not have written this story. Moore's thesis subsequently received support, however, from Anne Molet-Sauvaget, an expert on Madagascar, and is now widely accepted. Michel Le Bris, for example, in a fine preface to a recent new edition of *A General History*, attributed it to Daniel Defoe.

This confirmation, however, leads to a further mystery. How on earth could Defoe, who rarely left London, obtain such extensive documentation? In his book *Long John Silver*, the Swedish novelist Björn Larsson put forward a theory that is as preposterous as it is appealing. London's Execution Dock was graced by a tavern that went

LEFT
Illustration by Gustave Alaux for *The Treasure of Boquiseco*, by A. T'Sterstevens.

BELOW
Jack Avery in the Peck of Silver tavern, in *Illustrated history of pirates, corsairs, freebooters, buccaneers, slave traders and brigands from all ages and all countries*, by Jules Trousset, 1891.

RIGHT
Borgnefesse in his old age, in *Notebooks of Louis Adhémar Timothée le Golif, known as Borgnefesse*.

OVERLEAF
Generous treatment of Captain Desse, from Bordeaux, towards the "Columbus", a Dutch ship in the storm, by Théodore Gudin (1802–1880).

BORONEFESSE
dans
son vieil âge

by the curious name *Angel Pub* and had an excellent view of the gallows. This pub was extremely popular; it attracted common folk, ghouls, lawyers and judges. Customers could drink a pint or two of beer and, on most days, there was the added attraction of a hanging. Pirates who were still free to walk the streets also enjoyed these ceremonies, and came to watch their colleagues from the Caribbean or the Bahamas squirming at the end of a rope. Maybe they evaluated the courage of their dubious friends in their last brush with the law, or perhaps they searched for models of behaviour that they themselves could adopt when it was their turn for the scaffold.

According to Larsson's novel, one of the regulars in this dive had a particularly striking appearance. "He stood out from the rest. He wore a wig, but it was badly combed and in bad condition, his face was powdered – fairly unevenly, it must be said – and he had piles of paper set in front of him". This slightly greying old man used to watch the executions, and he struck up conversations with the

other customers. When he introduced himself, he started by saying he was called Johnson and then, after another pint, he would reveal his true identity: "My name is Defoe". He went on to explain. "I am preparing a book on pirates, the first ever description of their crimes and sins". So, it was by listening to drunks and women in this tavern that Daniel Defoe accumulated his vast knowledge of the brigands of the sea.

It might be objected that Björn Larsson is a novelist and that novelists lie all the time. In this case, however, Larsson is telling the truth: Defoe was indeed the author of *A general history of the robberies and murders of the most notorious pirates*. Are we then to believe that simply made up the chapter about Misson, Carracioli and Libertalia? It is here that another debate unfolds. Some critics claim that a writer as gifted as Defoe would not take the liberty of deceitfully inserting a tall story into a text that is otherwise very solid, with information that is all confirmed by eye-witness accounts or written sources. By contrast, others

maintain that Defoe was, above all, a poet of the first order, not a historian. His imagination was fertile, and he invented things as he wrote. He gave to the world a host of fictitious characters who seemed so real that they ended up claiming a place in history. Moreover, he enjoyed mixing true and false, to such an extent that the frontier between the two became blurred. Sometimes, it was the character forged by Defoe's lively mind that crossed into the land of reality. On other occasions, the opposite was the case: the person who had really lived took on the trappings of dreams and lies. Robinson Crusoe, the fruit of Defoe's reveries, has taken the place of a man who really existed, the sailor Alexander Selkirk, who was abandoned on the desert island of Juan Fernandez, and who has since disappeared from view because he was squeezed dry by the fictional hero that Defoe created out of his mishaps: Robinson Crusoe. Today, Crusoe is real, Selkirk is the dream. So, perhaps Defoe used similar methods in *A general history of the robberies and murders of the most notorious pirates* but pushed them to even greater extremes, in that Captain Misson did not need any historical support to come to life. He was a "virtual" pirate, but more real than any real pirate. He was entirely a figment of Defoe's imagination,

with no historical model. By breathing reality into the unreal, Defoe craftily sought to both confirm and undermine the activities of pirates, and maybe even teasingly call into question the reality of all creation and of Man himself.

There is another possible line of argument: Defoe was not only a superb writer, a virtuoso of the imagination, but also a highly perceptive philosopher. By this reckoning, *Robinson Crusoe* is, under the guise of an entertaining yarn for young and old alike, a lively but extremely malicious philosophy lesson that covers nature, culture, history, industry, tolerance, good and evil, savagery and civilisation, as well as what is "real" and what lies beyond this reality. In this case, the same would be true of the episode of Captain Misson and his republic of Libertalia. Defoe had wanted to broaden the scope of his scrupulously documented history of piracy by smuggling onboard a stowaway, entrusted with the mission of exploding the barnacled and dilapidated old boat of historical "truth", in order to create an historical fable focussing on the same themes as *Robinson Crusoe*: history, nature and culture, utopia and the return to Eden.

Furthermore, this fable about Paradise Lost works both as a tonic and an eye-opener. The sublime music of this hymn to freedom and goodness, its

Percy R Craft

The dandies of death

Bartholomew Roberts was a poor Welsh child who grew up to become a sailor in the early 18th century. In 1719 he started to take part in the slave trade on the coasts of Africa. He soon tired of this, however, and formed his own squadron of four well-armed ships that perpetrated dastardly deeds on both sides of the Atlantic – from Canada, the Caribbean and São Salvador de Bahia to Benin, Nigeria and Gabon. It is estimated that Roberts captured or sunk four hundred ships.

His career, like those of Teach and Lewis, was marked by cynicism, uncouthness and a devotion to barbarity. As he hated the French, he cut off their ears – except when he tied them to a mast and used them for shooting practice. These vile practices were brought to an end in 1722, when two English men-of-war intercepted his ship, the *Royal Fortune*, off Cape Lopez, in Gabon.

On the previous day the *Royal Fortune* had made a good haul and the crew, who had been celebrating, were tired and the worse for wear from drink. Bartholomew Roberts fought valiantly for three hours before falling under a hail of gunshot.

This character would not deserve to be described at any greater length if his savagery had not been accompanied by a few idiosyncrasies. He was a very handsome man – tall, dark and strikingly stylish. He wore a jacket and breeches made of

OPPOSITE
Illustration by Edward A. Wilson for *The pirate's treasure, a tale of Spanish Main*, 1926.

ABOVE
Illustration by Pablo Tillac in *Basque and Bayonnais corsairs from the 15th to 19th centuries*, by Pierre Rectoran, 1946.

BELOW
Illustration by Louis Marque for "The Gold-Bug" by Edgar Allan Poe.

A. Debelle del.   Huart sc.

high-quality damask, a hat adorned with a scarlet feather, a gold chain round his neck and a large diamond cross. The pistols from which he was never separated were kept in a shoulder belt made of silk.

Roberts only drank tea. He loved music but, as he claimed to be a religious man, he gave his musicians a day off on Sundays. Moreover, his ferocity was tempered by some bizarre religious scruples. When he was ravaging the coasts of Guinea in 1721, he captured a priest. Roberts begged him to become his chaplain but to no avail. Roberts decided to spare the priest anyway, but could not resist the temptation of stealing three prayer books and a corkscrew from him.

Roberts' taste for fine clothes was not uncommon among pirates. In the early 18th century, for example, there was a Dutch pirate in Madagascar called John Pro, who had no stockings or shoes but always wore a coat gleaming with jewels and silver buttons.

Later on, in the early 19th century, one de Soto, who operated off the coasts of Africa, dazzled his crew with his sophisticated clothing. According to one chronicler, "he usually wore a white hat, in the best English style, silk stockings, white breeches and a blue coat. His moustache was thick and bushy and his hair, which was very long, black and curly, gave him an air of a London preacher with prophetic and somewhat poetic tendencies. He was tanned by the sun and had an appearance and bearing that conveyed his pride, enterprise and readiness for anything."

In the 16th century, a certain Coia Acem, who cruised the seas of Japan, "wore a ribbed, knitted jacket lined with crimson satin and trimmed with a golden fringe". The appearance of one of the last known pirates, the American Eli Boggs, astonished the *Times* correspondent who spotted him in the China Seas around 1850: "It was impossible to believe that this pretty boy with carefully combed hair, a feminine face, a charming smile and delicate hands could be the man whose name had been associated with the most audacious and bloody acts of piracy."

This predilection for dandyism shared by so many pirates served to unite them with other groups of rebels, reprobates or dicers with death. Spanish bullfighters spend hours putting on their costume. The fearsome Brazilian bandits of the early 20th century, the *cangaceiros*, decorated their cocked hats with dozens of golden coins. They were so fond of lace and trimmings that their chief, Lampeao, never took on a right-hand man

Jolly Roger

The insignia of a pirate is a black flag emblazoned with a white skull and crossbones. This is how the pirate flag has been represented for the last two centuries, on the basis of the tales of Walter Scott and Robert Louis Stevenson.

The reality is rather more complicated. Firstly, the pirate flag was not always black; other colours can be used, especially red. There has been much debate as to which came first — black or red — but it is now generally agreed that the black flag was hoisted to warn an enemy that it was in his interests to surrender without a fight; it was the equivalent of a warning shot across the bows. The red flag was more forthright: it announced death.

The decorative motifs on the flag could also vary. The skull and crossbones were indeed often present, but they could be accompanied by other figures. Stede Bonnet rounded them off with a white heart. Blackbeard was more provocative: his flag displayed a skeleton with horns like a devil, an hourglass in one hand and, in the other, an arrow piercing a red heart with three big drops of blood falling from it. Thomas Tew opted for an arm holding a double-edged sword; this proved premonitory, as Tew was decapitated by the sword of an Indian pirate in 1695. Pirates liked explicit symbols: blood, skulls, bones, swords, cannonballs with a lighted fuse, etc; the whole panoply of death graced their flags. The use of the hourglass is more ambiguous. Some experts claim that it warned an enemy ship that it did not have long to survive; for others, it referred to the pirate as much as the enemy: it declared that life is fleeting and made of sand.

The pirate who, above all others, brought flag design to perfection was the dandy Bartholomew Roberts. He loved to dress up and he appreciated music and painting. He was a sophisticate, a poet, and his flag formed part of the work of art that he wanted to make out of his own life. That is why he produced several models of flags. The most famous one depicted a man armed with a sword treading on two skulls. Under one of these skulls were the three letters ABH, meaning A Barbadian Head; under the other, AMH, which denoted A Martinican Head, in recognition of his thirst for vengeance against the islands of Barbados and Martinica, which had recently brought complications into his life. Sometimes he adopted other themes, such as a pirate sharing a toast with death.

The pirate flag is known as the Jolly Roger. For years, historians have racked their brains in an attempt to unravel the origin of this name, and some etymologists have admitted defeat. The most widely accepted theory, however, is that the French filibusters, when they saw the red flag of their English counterparts, dubbed it a "joli rouge", and that this term became corrupted to "Jolly Roger" when it was later adopted by English pirates.

More exotic origins have also been suggested, namely the East Indies, where there was a great pirate chief called Ali Raja, which means "king of the sea". Other pirates, finding it interesting, assumed a corruption of the nickname for themselves.

Is it really necessary to choose between these versions? Let us close the debate without any further ado!

Piratenflaggen aus der Blütezeit der westindischen Seeräuber um 1700

Kapitän Roberts

Schwarzbart

Long Ben

Major Bonnet

Calico Jack

Pavillons pirates.

155

who was incapable of embroidering or using a sewing machine.

Baudelaire sensed the underlying seriousness of these curious links between death and coquetry, murder and elegance, when he described the dandyism of revolt: "all [these rebels] have the same origins, they all participate in the same way in opposition and revolt, they are all representatives of what is best in human pride, of that need, all too rare among those of today, to combat and destroy triviality. Dandyism is the last sparkle of revolt in decadence."

Another great writer, Emil Cioran, has put dandyism in its rightful place, which is that of nothingness, that nothingness which makes up the essence, obsessive fear and fascination of the pirate. "Clothing", wrote Cioran, "comes between us and nothingness. Look at your body in a mirror: you will understand that you're mortal; run your fingers along your sides, as if they were a mandolin, and you will see how close you are to the tomb. It is because we are dressed that we delude ourselves about immortality: how can anybody die if he is wearing a tie? The corpse that is decked out does not recognise itself and, imagining eternity, appropriates the illusion. Flesh covers the skeleton, clothes cover the flesh: subterfuges of Nature and Man, instinctive and conventional duperies: a gentleman could not be moulded out of mud or dust... Dignity, honour, decency – so many flights in the face of the irremediable. And, when you put on a hat, who would say that you have passed a spell among entrails or that worms will eat your fat?"

Women pirates

For a long time, historians claimed that piracy was a trade reserved for men, but this view has become outmoded. Is this an anachronistic effect of feminism? Did the pirates in the Seychelles apply the law of parity, three centuries in advance? In any case, the historians now assure us that, on the sly, the profession of piracy was adopted by several female freebooters and pirates. Some eminent authorities go much further. For Michel Le Bris, women were extremely common in pirate bands, not only on dry land but also on a number of pirate ships themselves.

One of the pioneers was a Swede called Alvilda, who created mayhem just before the year 1000. She deserves understanding; her parents wanted her to marry a Danish prince called Alf but, as she was not keen on this man at all, she took to sea,

with an all-female crew. Her exploits earned her a title: Alvilda the Terrible.

In France, Jeanne de Belleville was a woman of spirit. Her husband, the Seigneur de Clisson, a Chevalier from Nantes, was accused of conspiring with the English and accordingly beheaded in 1343. Mme de Clisson sold her furniture and jewellery, bought two ships and, taking her two sons with her, went on to take revenge by sinking ships belonging to the King of France.

The 17th century saw the rise of the Englishwoman Charlotte de Berry. As a young girl, her fantasies revolved around cutlasses, flint guns, bombards, skirmishes and blood. She married a sailor and dressed up as a man so that she could accompany him. Later on, she was the leader of the mutiny off the coast of Africa and became known as Captain Charlotte. Then it was anchors aweigh and full speed ahead to a life of pillage, fighting and Spanish gold.

In the last twenty years or so, however, a whole assortment of female stowaways has begun to emerge out of the holds of pirate vessels. In Virginia in the early 18th century, for example, there were Mary Harley and Mary Crickett. The latter was a particularly stubborn case: when her seafaring adventures brought her to court for the first time she was acquitted because she was a woman, but she immediately enlisted again on another ship. The judge at her second trial was not so charitable and sent her to the gallows. Later on in the century, the Englishwoman Ann Mills was

LEFT
The angel of the wind, illustration by Gustave Alaux in *The Pig boucan* by A. T'Sterstevens.

Literature and the cinema have both been fascinated by female pirates. The director Frédéric de Cordova made *The Daughter of Buccaneers* for the French star Yvonne de Carlo, while Hollywood pitched in with *Anne of the Indies*, directed by Jacques Tourneur and starring Jean Peters. These films do not always respect the strict historical truth; in *Anne of the Indies*, Ann Bonny is pitted against Blackbeard, even though the two never met in real life.

RIGHT
The two women corsairs or the two adulterous wives, an anonymous print illustrating a news story (1840).

LES DEUX FEMMES CORSAIRES,
OU LES DEUX ÉPOUSES ADULTÈRES.

responsible for several acts of war. On one occasion, she found herself in a hand-to-hand skirmish with a Frenchman; having run him through with her sword, she cut off his head to make sure he was dead.

Generally speaking, however, women pirates stuck to dry land – in the freebooter refuges, taverns and camps of the Caribbean, the Bahamas or the Mascarene Islands. The regulations onboard the ships were strict and forbade the intrusion of women – and any freebooter found having sex in the hold would be very severely punished. These prohibitions are not surprising. It is well known that the presence of women in a community of young, lusty, rustic bachelors sows disorder, fights and resentment. The scent of a woman does not mix well with the whiff of gunpowder.

There are more subtle reasons, too. For pirates, a ship was a space disinfected from the miasmas of the world, a domain devoted to other passions and other disciplines than those of history. As the Bible and the Fathers of the Church noted a long time ago, women suffer from an essential impurity. Any female presence in the closed world of a boat would have unsettled the perfect, black crystal of the pirate utopia. Pirates abandoned the sordidness of Europe to settle in the petrified present of heaven on earth, far from the convulsions of time – and it is on record that Edens do not resist for long the scheming of women.

On land, by contrast, a woman was neither out of place nor dangerous. In fact, she was eminently desirable. Above all, she was extremely useful for practical chores around the cabin and taking charge of the cooking of turtles, birds and eggs. Her sensuality did not threaten the order of pirate society as dry land, unlike the microcosm of a ship, was governed by the laws of history – those

159

laws that pirates dreamed of abolishing when they embarked for the end of the world. When a pirate returned to his camp and tavern after having sunk a galleon and tortured a few Spaniards, he was returning to the realm of history. There, a woman had a place and a role: was she not one of the protagonists of history and even its prime mover, if only because she produced children?

Pirates were not particularly fond of children, and preferred fornication to procreation. They rarely left any heirs. This trait confirms the fact that pirates had an obscure – and no doubt unconscious – design to desert the provinces of history and escape from the future. Pirates knew no yesterday or tomorrow. They were men of the present and their eternity was nothing more than an interminable present. Here we find yet another example of the ontological difference between the sacred enclosure of the ship – utopian and timeless – and the profane spaces of land – historical and subject to change. Pirates not only effaced their own parents and childhood, they also cut themselves from their offspring. If, by some mischance, they got a woman pregnant, the conception did not take place within the bounds of the ship but in a tavern, on land – and so they would not even know they had a child. Pirates remained faithful to the oath they swore to themselves: to

live without descendants. They answered only to death, which brought an abrupt halt not only to themselves but also their lineage.

The highly perceptive Jean-Jacques Rousseau wrote, in his *Discourse on the origin of languages*: "The profession of hunter is not favourable to the population. This observation that was made when the islands of Tortuga and Santo Domingo were inhabited by buccaneers is confirmed by the state of North America. We do not see the forefathers of any populous nation being hunters by nature; they have all been farmers or herdsmen."

Let us return to the women pirates. Some were highly flamboyant, particularly Mary Read and Ann Bonny, who were in the Caribbean in the early 18th century. Their adventures were just as thrilling as those of their male colleagues, but they also introduced into the rough-and-ready world of piracy the sparkle of doomed and illicit love.

Ann Bonny was the daughter of an Irish lawyer from Cork. As a girl, she was as pretty as an angel and as naughty as a devil. Her father left Europe to run a plantation in Charleston, Virginia, and made his fortune. The girl became a woman but her temperament did not soften. When a young man tried to woo her, Ann knocked him flat. Shortly afterwards, however, she was seduced by a sailor. She knew that he was worthless, but she married him, bid farewell to her rich father, headed for the Caribbean, disguised herself as a man and opted for a life full of sound and fury. In Providence, in 1719, she fell under the spell of a wild, romantic English pirate called Calico Jack Rackham, known for his trademark red breeches. As the two young people were not sure where to get married, they stole a brig and performed the ceremony on the deck. This brig proved very useful, as it served them to wreak havoc among the merchants in the area for several years.

Through an extraordinary coincidence, another cross-dressing woman also formed part of Calico Jack's band: Mary Read. She was illegitimate, born in a poverty-stricken suburb of London. Her mother's husband was not her father. Her mother dressed her as a boy, in memory of an older brother who had previously died. The young Mary did not object as she loved playing and getting into scraps. She briefly enlisted in the Navy, dressed as a boy, and then maintained her disguise to become a soldier in Flanders. One of her companions in arms uncovered her true identity and, fascinated,

married her, before promptly dying. Mary made her way to the Netherlands. She joined another regiment but was soon out of a job because an armistice was declared. At her wits' ends, she signed on with a Dutch ship heading for America but was captured by pirates en route. She was soon sharing their life and demonstrating her ferocity. Her military experience in both Belgium and Holland stood her in good stead. She loved duelling pirate-style, with a short epée in one hand and a pistol in the other. Like Ann Bonny, she had some seafaring romances. One day, her lover at the time was provoked on a beach by a famous and pitiless swashbuckler. Mary's lover was out of his class and was killed, whereupon Mary set about violently berating the murderous brute. He lost his temper and challenged her to a duel, but this time it was his turn to be outclassed. Calico Jack's ship, now with both women onboard, had caused so much trouble in the sea round Jamaica that the Governor of the Bahamas, Woodes Rogers, decided to hunt it down. The fateful encounter took place in 1720. The pirates

Ann Bonny *and* Mary Read *convicted of Piracy Nov.* 28th *1720 at a Court of Vice Admiralty held at* St Jago de la Vega *in y Island of Jamaica.*

161

another legend invented by Captain Johnson, or the wily Daniel Defoe, considered responsible, in some quarters, for dreaming up the Malagasy utopia of Misson and Carracioli. Although Captain Johnson remains the primary source of information, however, numerous documents confirm the two women's epic adventures, particularly legal records and contemporary accounts of their trial published in reputable newspapers. These articles are extremely revealing and serve to fill in the gaps left by Defoe's sketch. They tell us, for example, that, although they wore men's clothes while fighting, they reverted to female attire when peace was restored. Their ferocity, their mad courage and even their cruelty were stressed in all the commentaries.

Finally, as we have seen, they had active sex lives. Some witnesses described them as debauched, and when their tempers rose they were prone to use obscene language.

Hubert Deschamps recounts one particularly spicy episode. He claims that Ann Bonny, when she first set eyes on the disguised Mary Read, imagined that this young sailor must have been a fine figure of a man under his clothing and fell in love with him. The young cross-dressed woman declared her passion to the other young cross-dressed woman. Mary Read played her along for a while, before explaining "that she was not in the condition to satisfy her as she was a woman in disguise". They found the situation amusing – besides, they both had plenty of other sailors at their disposal – and a deep, lasting friendship grew up between the two women. Another great historian of piracy, Philip Gosse, does not, however, mention this touching scene, which seems to have come straight out of Shakespeare or Marivaux.

Mary Read had firm convictions about the profession of piracy. She maintained that, to exercise it with honour, it was necessary to be like her, "a courageous man". When she was questioned at

LEFT
Duel of Mary Read in *Illustrated history of pirates, corsairs, freebooters, buccaneers, slave traders and brigands from all ages and all countries,* by Jules Trousset, 1891.

RIGHT
Mary Read, illustration by Debelle in *History of pirates and corsairs of the ocean and the Mediterranean, from their origin to the present* by P. Christian, 1846.

"The French Revolution: they had no more ancestors and few relatives. They did not grow old. When Saint-Just saw Hoche for the last time, they were both twenty-six. Danton died at the age of thirty-five, Robespierre thirty-six... No family: a destiny forged by the hands of men; and, in the period when Saint-Just had his greatest power, no women."
André Malraux

had been living it up the night before and they were, as so often, hopelessly drunk. Their courage deserted them and they slunk away like rats to hide in the hold. Only the two women remained on deck, having first fired a few shots at their cowardly companions. They fought against the English but were outnumbered.

The entire band was taken to Jamaica to stand trial. Many of them were sentenced to death, but Mary Read and Ann Bonny were spared as they had managed to get themselves pregnant. The two women were therefore able to attend the execution of Calico Jack and their other comrades. Ann Bonny was asked for her impressions as she watched her lover climb up to the scaffold. She said she was heartbroken to see him there, but went on to add a caveat: "But if he had fought like a lion, he would not be in the position of being hanged like a dog." (An alternative version has her saying: "But if he had fought like a man, ...").

The story of these two women is so enthralling that it has sometimes been thought that it was yet

The law onboard a pirate ship

For the pirate — who despised earthly laws and turned them upside down the day he left the King's service to serve under the Jolly Roger — the law was no joking matter, when that law was his own. Order reigned on the rebel ships. The freebooters were in advance of all the European monarchies; absolute power did not exist in piracy. The exercise of tyranny was unknown, and a captain was subject to the same law as his crew. The regulations set up a delicate balance between rights, duties and powers, worthy of Montesquieu. Two centuries before Rousseau, criminals in the Caribbean invented the "social contract". Pirate regulations were striking for their combination of high-mindedness and implacability, as can be seen from those of the *Revenge*, which used to attack the fishermen of Newfoundland:

"Every man must obey the courteous laws; the captain will have one and a half parts of all the prizes; the skipper, shipwright, boatswain and gunner will have one and a quarter parts.

Any man who proposes deserting or keeping something hidden from the brotherhood will be abandoned on land with a bottle of powder, a bottle of water, a small arm and ammunition.

Any man who steals anything from the brotherhood or who gambles for a value of at least one piastre will be abandoned on land or shot.

At any time that we meet another pirate, the man who would sign the present articles without the consent of our brotherhood will undergo the punishment that the captain and the brotherhood consider appropriate.

Any man who strikes another while the present articles are in force will be subject to the application of the law of Moses (that is forty blows minus one) on his bare back.

Any man who breaks his arms, or who smokes tobacco in the hold without having put a guard on his pipe, or who bears a lighted candle outside a lantern will be submitted to the treatment laid down in the previous article.

Any man who does not have his arms in a condition ready for service, or who neglects his post, will be deprived of his share and will be subjected to any other judgement that the caption and the brotherhood consider appropriate.

Any man who loses a joint in combat will receive four hundred piastres. If it is a limb, eight hundred. If at any moment any one of you find yourselves in the presence of an honest woman, any man who wants to constrain her will immediately be put to death."

It is plain to see that democracy, morality and sexual harassment are not taken lightly onboard a pirate vessel.

Oexmelin wrote: "The pirates observe the most perfect order among themselves [...].

There are some who are very courteous and very charitable, to the point that if one has need of a thing that is possessed by another, he offers it to him with generosity."

Oexmelin stressed that pirate regulations were respected to the letter — at least onboard a ship. On land, with the presence of rum, revelry and women, it was a different matter. Land was the opposite of the sea.

"Truth on this side of the shore, error beyond."

RIGHT
Torture scene.

BELOW
Horrible abuses committed
against defenceless women in
the cabin, in *The pirate's own
book*, 1837.

her trial about the matter of the death penalty, she put forward the very reasonable argument that:

"it was not a useless penalty, for, if it did not exist, all the worthless people would become pirates and would infest the sea to such a degree that the only thing open to good-hearted people would be dying of hunger."

In the China Seas

Madame Ching was an uncouth woman with a face like a bear. "Her eyes were dull and her teeth were rotten. Her oily, black hair shined more than her eyes." Nevertheless, she had plenty of people under her command: five hundred junks ranging from fifteen to two hundred tons, the biggest ones equipped with twenty-five cannons. These vessels were divided into six squadrons, instantly recognisable by the colour and design of their flags – red, green, violet, yellow, black and, finally, a snake motif.

Madame Ching gave the commanders of her squadrons some very pretty nicknames. Her trusted lieutenants were not called Peg-Leg, Big Thighbone or Cut Nose, but rather Bird and Flint, Jewel of All the Crew, Scourge of the Morning Sea, Meadow of Frogs, High Sun or Wave Full of Fish. Such refinement was not in evidence, however, onboard the junks. The holds where the sailors slept were squalid, and their diet consisted of force-fed rats, caterpillars and rice. They prepared for battle by anointing their bodies with garlic. In quieter moments, they passed the time playing cards or dice and smoking opium.

In 1808 Madame Ching engaged in a deadly battle with an imposing fleet that the Emperor sent to pacify the coasts of southern China. The battle was ruthless and, as is traditional on these occasions, ended up with the sea stained a bloody red and dotted with corpses. The pirates, however, came out the winners.

During the course of the battle, Paou, a chubby young man who was one of Madame Ching's commanders, captured the Emperor's admiral, the venerable Kwo Lang. The humiliated admiral felt dishonoured and searched for a means to die. He grabbed hold of Paou by the hair and scowled in his face, in the hope that the young man would

BELOW
The Port of Canton,
by Thomas Daniel.

RIGHT
Cargo of tea onboard a boat, under the vigilance of a European, painting on silk, late 18th century.

I've painted my boat
With China ink,
The anchor is made of iron,
The salt rusts it,
And in China
My straw boat
Will be wrecked.

OVERLEAF
Gulf of Tschili, (China), by James Baylie Allen, after Thomas Allom.

Traditionally, the pirates in China were Tankas, very poor, small-scale fishermen who were greatly despised by the Imperial administration. Later on, in the 15th century, the Tankas joined forces with Japanese adventurers, known as the Wokou, who went on to comprise 35% of the total Chinese numbers. The Chinese fought with a long, heavy sword, capable of cutting through armour plating in the hands of an expert. The Japanese used swords that were lighter but no less dangerous; the Wokou wielded them with dazzling dexterity, whirring the blades around their body like flashes of lightning.

LEFT
Macao.

RIGHT
French steamboat attacked by
Chinese pirates, *Le Petit Journal*,
12 June 1913.

Europe showed great interest in
China. They did not seek to
colonise it; instead, they tried to
take advantage of its wealth by
dominating its trade. In the 16th
century, Portugal and Holland
were already fighting over the
rich pickings. The Dutch were
well received by the Chinese,
who admired their practical
spirit and their disdain for all
religious proselytism. In 1624
they were given the right to
settle in Taiwan, where they
encouraged piracy among some
poor communities. They
eventually monopolised all the
major trading posts in southern
China. The Portuguese, for their
part, laid their hands on Macao,
at the mouth of the "River of
Pearls", a veritable haven of
pirates and open smugglers. It
went on to inflame European
imaginations with its gaming
houses, women and opium dens.

BELOW
Pair of Chinese swords from the
mid-19th century.

Madame Ching issued orders that submitted her
underlings to a draconian moral code. "If a man
goes on land on his own account, or if he commits
the act known as "crossing the barriers", he will
have his ears pierced in front of the whole fleet; in
case of recidivism, he will be put to death. [...] It is
forbidden to take, in a personal capacity, the slightest part of the booty arising from theft and pillage.
Everything will be registered and the pirate will
receive two parts out of ten for him, while the
other eight parts will belong to the store called
"the general fund"; taking anything from this general fund will entail death [...] Nobody must
behave licentiously for his own pleasure with the
women captured in villages or the country and
brought onboard a ship. Permission must first be
requested from the steward, and the woman must
then be taken into the ship's hold. The use of violence towards a woman without the steward's permission will be punished with death."

The confederation was dissolved after a few years,
but this did not put a stop to Chinese piracy. The
junks stalked new prey, in the form of the large,
rich European ships that crisscrossed the Far East.
The Opium War raged from 1839 to 1842, but the
British had a decisive technical advantage – steam
engines – that prevented the junks from getting
out of range in time.

In 1849, the English attacked *Shap'n'gtzai*, reputedly the greatest of all Oriental vessels. She took
refuge in the mouth of the Haiphong River, in
northern Vietnam, and prepared for a counter
attack. The tide came up, however, and the cur-
rent turned, displacing the Chinese ship without
giving the crew time to re-aim their cannons. This
proved to be the last chapter in the epic of
Chinese piracy.

Death without burial

For these men "without god or law", death was their sovereign. The pirates' thrilling exploits were nothing more than indefatigable perdition. Their violence and pleasure, their festivities, their plundering and killing, every moment of their existence was caressed by the lonely rays of death. This death was something they distributed with largesse: "In the republic of pirates", wrote the surgeon Oexmelin, "he who commits the most crimes is regarded as an extraordinary individual." Some pirates openly admitted their relish for killing. In the 17th century, for example, John Ward mourned the passing of Elizabeth I in these terms: "Under her reign, one could sing, swear, give out a good hiding and kill men as freely as your bakers make pies."

The captains of rebel ships were often gross (Blackbeard, Fly, Avery and countless others) but their crews were usually more than able to live down to their standards, as we can see from the images of Low's or the Olonnais's men slaughtering their prisoners. They look as if they are dancing, with a slightly malicious but mischievous and childlike air. They knew that they themselves would encounter death soon; as the dandy Bartholomew Roberts proclaimed, "A short but happy life; that will be my motto."

Death was so familiar and their days were so similar that they used murder as a way of entertaining themselves. In the times of the freebooters, when the food was even worse than usual, the cook would be caught and set alight on deck, "to see the beautiful fire made by all his fat and grime".

Blackbeard invented a game that could be called "pirate roulette". When the days were particularly long, he shut himself in the hold with his sailors and let off a volley of shots at random. After that, they counted the dead and wounded As Oexmelin said, "Alive today, dead tomorrow, who cares about saving and housekeeping, what matters to us is the day we are living, never the one we shall have to live."

They seemed unperturbed by the gallows that awaited them on the docks of London or a beach in Ecuador. In fact, they used to joke about, saying "I'll dance a jig on the end of a rope". One pirate dreamed of the day "when they bless the soil with my feet". Another joked about his failing health: "I'm becoming so thin that if this must last any longer, I fear that my body may not be heavy enough to pull on the knot of the rope".

Not that all pirates died on the scaffold – far from it. More often than not, they fell in the course of a battle or were drowned in a shipwreck, and a good few perished on the desert island where they were abandoned with their bottle of gunpowder, bottle of water, gun and bullets, without anything even to light a fire.

Although the pirate's roads to death were varied and unpredictable, one factor was constant: they only rarely reached old age. They died young, on the job, with the exception of a few illustrious

LEFT
The Hanged Man "Ecce"
by Victor Hugo, brown wash with highlights in white.

ABOVE
Illustration by Pablo Tillac from *Basque and Bayonnais corsairs from the 15th to 19th centuries*, by Pierre Rectoran, 1946.

Human brothers who are born after us,
Do not have hearts hardened against us,
For, if you have pity on us,
God will give you mercies sooner.
You see attached here five, six;
As for the flesh, which we have nourished too much,
It is no more,
devoured and rotten,
And we, the bones,
become ash and powder.
Let nobody laugh at our sad state,
But pray to God, for His grace to absolve us all.
François Villon,
The ballad of the hanged men

LEFT AND BELOW
Illustrations by Pablo Tillac from
*Basque and Bayonnais corsairs
from the 15th to 19th centuries,*
by Pierre Rectoran, 1946.

RIGHT
The head of Herman Ruyter,
nailed all black on a gallows in
*Illustrated history of pirates,
corsairs, freebooters, buccaneers,
slave traders and brigands from
all ages and all countries,*
by Jules Trousset, 1891.

Of all human communities, whether sophisticated or primitive, the pirate community was one of the few that never dreamed of creating orders, medals or honours, or of founding libraries, towns, monuments or cemeteries. These people without diaries or archives left no children behind them. They chose to live and die without memories. Prehistoric men buried their dead. "There is probably no society", wrote Claude Lévi-Strauss, "that does not treat its death with consideration. At the frontiers of the species, Neanderthal man buried his dead in rudimentary tombs" – which was more than the pirate did, placing him beyond "the frontiers of the species".

When a pirate died at sea, his companions chucked him overboard and that was the end of the story. The most common punishment was hanging. This followed protocols. In British territories, the scaffold was set up on the foreshore and, following the directives of the Admiralty, the ceremony always took place at low tide, so that the corpses could be swept out to sea at high tide. Landlubbers thoroughly enjoyed these macabre spectacles. When Stede Bonnet was executed in Charleston in 1725, the docks were overflowing with people, and the audience had an added extra

examples, like Henry Morgan, the freebooter turned policeman, or the old man of Corcyrus so entertainingly described in the *Bucolics* of Virgil. Pirates' last moments were calm and rarely caused them to be overcome with emotion. Pirates advanced towards their end as if they were going to greet an old acquaintance. Nothingness had been their most enduring companion, their familiar shadow and the organiser of their pleasures. Several chronicles describe the death of a pirate, and the dominant note is one of great simplicity. Obviously, there were a few pretentious rascals who made an exhibition of themselves, such as Bartholomew Roberts, who maintained his dandyish posturing right to the gallows, but most of them accepted the verdict stoically. They had played a diabolical game; for a long time, they had won; now they had lost, and that was all there was to it. They were not going to make a song and dance about it. They were not rebellious, angry or astonished. They smiled when it was time for their execution, just as – according to Chateaubriand – the Barbary pirates used to do. At the foot of the scaffold, they turned up at the appointment that they had made with truth a long time before. Their day was done. They left the sea, women, gold and the sun. They left behind them neither memoirs nor melancholy nor posterity. Their life was undone, and the wind of God would erase their footprints from the sand.

A pirate captain falls

"The next day Davis went on shore himself, as if it were out of greater respect to bring the governor on board. He was received with the usual civility, and he, and other principal pirates, who, by the way, had assumed the title of lords, and as such took upon them to advise or counsel their captain upon any important occasion; and likewise held certain privileges, which the common pirates were debarred from, as walking the quarter deck, using the great cabin, going ashore at pleasure, and treating with foreign powers, that is, with the captains of ships they made prize of; I say, Davis and some of the lords were desired to walk up to the governor's house, to take some refreshment before they went on board; they accepted it without the least suspicion, but never returned again; for an ambush was laid, a signal being given, a whole volley was fired upon them; they every man dropped, except one ... Davis was shot through the bowels, yet he rose again, and made a weak effort to get away, but his strength soon forsook him, and he dropped down dead; just as he fell, he perceived he was followed, and drawing out his pistols, fired them at his pursuers; thus like a game cock, giving a dying blow that he might not fall unavenged." Captain Charles Johneson/Daniel Defoe.

because the condemned man had to wait for several hours at the foot of the scaffold for a pardon from the Governor – that never arrived.

Mutilation and public display of corpses were used by governments as a deterrent for young boys tempted to depart from the straight and narrow. William Kidd was hanged in London in 1701. The first rope broke in two, so another one was brought. When Kidd was finally dead, his corpse was exhibited on Tilbury Point, in order to intimidate all the boats sailing on the Thames. His body had previously been coated with tar, to prevent it from decomposing too quickly and thereby prolonging the cautionary lesson. In other cases, a pirate's body was attached to the prow of one of the king's ships. The head of Blackbeard, which had hardly been a pretty sight when he was alive, served as an ornament for his conqueror's bowsprit for many a day.

The authorities were sometimes concerned that friends of the deceased might steal a displayed body and therefore destroy its symbolic power. So they shut the body up in a steel cage, reminiscent of a woman's corset, in order to keep the bones in position, even after the flesh had putrefied. The Admiralty wanted to make sure that pirates did not have a decent tomb.

Even monks, in their enclosed retreats, used to water the rose trees growing out of the tombs of their departed brothers, but pirates wanted nothing of roses or tears. They never dreamed of bestowing nobility or emotion on their demise. A pirate went away, that was all, and no posterity would keep his memory alive.

Now, the pirate era is no more. These men sailed for a brief moment under forbidden moons; they left neither tombstones nor children nor archives. They were barbaric or brotherly, perverse or merciful, heroic or cowardly. They may instil contempt and hatred, but their nobility was to die without vanity. Their booty is lost for ever and no epitaph will ever celebrate their memory. They lived to die, on the margins of history. All we sense of their deserted hideouts, their loves and their drunkenness, is the undertow of nothingness. The pirate civilisation can never be buried.

M. ORANGE

C·1

•
747.2
Mc
McCreary
Havens II: celebrity lfiestyles

6-99   8-00B

When I feel the need to get away from the hustle and bustle of city life, I go off to my home

in Santa Fe. My dear friend and interior designer, Anita Ludovici De Domenico, has captured

Southwest Adobe architecture and all it has to offer.

I love all the rooms in my home, but if I had to pick just one room as my

favorite, it would have to be my bathroom. It's the place where I can hang for

hours, whether I'm relaxing in the tub with a glowing fire, reading a great

book, putting on my face in the mirror, or just sitting in the director's chair—

which has "Kalola" inscribed on it, meaning Carol in Hawaiian—deciding

what to wear. It's the place where I can be alone and have some time for myself.

One of the highlights I like to show friends who come to

visit me for the first time is the trompe l'oeil painting in

*O*ur home is our retreat from the world—our temple, our safe haven, where we can get in touch with

each other and our children.

Julia and I wanted to bring elements into the interiors that feel

sensual and earthy, sexy and sentimental. I want our home to be

a comfortable, loving environment, a reflection and reminder

of who we are. Because we now have five children, our first rule

is that our home must be kid friendly. And on the flip side of

that, I also need a quiet zone to write, meditate, and relax.

Our bedroom serves us both in that way. I wanted it to feel like our sacred space, a room that unabashedly celebrates

our love. So, quite naturally, the "mega-family bed" sort of

grew from that as well.

The W.C. door is an acid-etched tribute to the Big Sur,

California, coastline, one of the places where we first fell

in love. This is the bathroom where Julia and I wrote a

lot of our book, The Unimaginable Life. *I knew it would be*

cozy when I added the slate and paned windows, but

I didn't expect to live in it.

Kenny & Julia Loggins

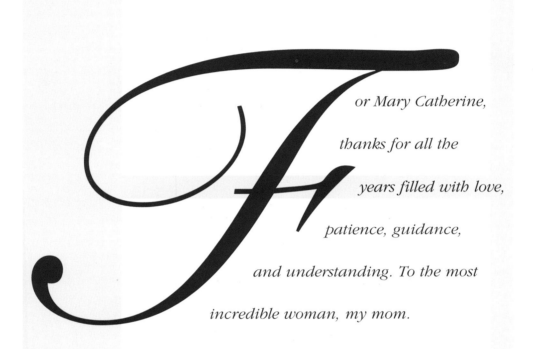

For Mary Catherine, thanks for all the years filled with love, patience, guidance, and understanding. To the most incredible woman, my mom.

With love and heartfelt appreciation to the following individuals and companies, without whose talent, generosity, care, and support, this book would not have been possible.

Executive Producer

AVA FARENTINO

Producer

JOHN M. COX IV

Assistants to the Photographer

DON SHETTERLY

KENNY TALLIER

ACKNOWLEDGMENTS

PUBLIC RELATIONS

BAKER WINOKUR RYDER: Mary Kaye Daniels

THE BECKWITH COMPANY: David Beckwith

BRAGMAN NYMAN CAFARELLI: Brad Cafarelli
Susan Dubow

THE BROKAW COMPANY: Joel Brokaw

WARREN COWAN & ASSOCIATES: Liza Anderson
Monica Rivas

LORI DE WAAL & ASSOCIATES: Lori De Waal

FELDMAN PUBLIC RELATIONS: Brenda Feldman

DICK GUTTMAN & ASSOCIATES: Dick Guttman
Rona Menashe

THE JIM HENSON COMPANY PUBLIC RELATIONS:
Dolores Richardone

HOPE ENTERPRISES: Public/Media Relations
Ward Grant

HUVANE•BAUM•HALL: Dominique Appel

JONAS PUBLIC RELATIONS, INC.: Jeff Abraham,
Andi Schechter

JOOP!: Director Public Relations: Arthur Wayne

KALEIDOSCOPE MEDIA: Angie Gore

KELMAN & BURDITCH: Deborah Kelman

ROGERS & COWAN: Julie Nathanson, Jill Bushinsky,
Michelle Bega

SEA WORLD OF CALIFORNIA PUBLIC RELATIONS:
Kina Scudi

KEITH SHERMAN & ASSOCIATES, INC.:
Anna Suslovski

RACHAEL VIZCARRA PUBLIC RELATIONS:
Rachael Vizcarra

WOLF-KASTELER: Annett Wolf, Lisa Kasteler,
Mia Ricchiuti, Marla Weinstein

MANAGEMENT

BAUMGARTEN/PROPHET ENTERTAINMENT:
Melissa Prophet

BRIAN BOITANO ENTERPRISES: Linda Leaver

HOFFLUND/PALONE: Gavin Palone, Tom Demko

KROST/CHAPIN MANAGEMENT: Kenny Iwamasa

MICHAEL LEVINE MANAGEMENT: Michael Levine

COVER PHOTO DESIGN: John Johnson

COVER and BACK COVER PHOTOS: Home of John
Paul and Eloise DeJoria

SPECIAL THANKS: Nancy Sills, Carla Fagan,
Dan Karslake, Russ Anderson, Mark Arden,
George Richey, Deirdre Richardson, Ga Shull,
Laurie Hartman, John Paul and Eloise DeJoria,
Jo-Anne Wallace, Michael Levine, Ward Grant,
Dolores Richardone, Angie Gore, Ken Farrar

MISS PIGGY'S BATHROOM: Home of Jo-Anne Wallace
Stylist: Jane Gootnick, Writer: Jim Lewis

SHAMU'S TRAINERS: Jeff Andrews, Lisa Hugueley

BRIAN BOITANO'S MEDAL PHOTO: Cheryl Fenton

HAIR: Maria Conchita Alonso–Sergio Lopez,
Carol Burnett–Sachi Worall

MAKE-UP:
Maria Conchita Alonso–Sergio Lopez
Carol Burnett–Brenda Todd
Swoosie Kurtz–Adam Christopher

INTERIOR DESIGNERS:
Carol Burnett–Anita Ludovici De Domenico
Brooke Shields–Maude MacGillivray, Inc. ASID
Renee Taylor–Terry Landeck: Project Manager

ARCHITECTS:
Swoosie Kurtz–Christopher Carr of Wiehle Carr

CELEBRITY PORTRAITS:
Cher–Michael Lavine
Roy Disney–John Galuzzi
Wolfgang Joop–Gabo
Cheech Marin–Courtesy of CBS-TV
Priscilla Presley–Bernd Boehm
Melody Thomas Scott–Courtesy of CBS-TV
Brooke Shields–Walter Chin
Kenny Loggins–Jeremiah Sullivan

THANK YOU: Constanza Arango, Art Baer, Randy Ball,
Peggy Bass, Leon Carroll, Thomas Castaneda, Jeanine Chan,
Steven B. Clark, Jeff Collins, Kay Collins, Michael Connor,
Jenna Copozzi, C & S RV & Truck, Chris Cummings,
Hollie Dickinson, Mohamed Diop, Glenda Duke,
John Evatz, Tony Farentino, Trudy Farley, Cheryl Fenton,
Susy Fontana, Chris Gallucci, Brandi Glanville,
Jane Gootnick, Robert Greening, Susan Grushkin,
Toni Holliday, John Johnson, Bonnie Kim, Rita Kohler,
Terry Landeck, Jennifer Lewis, Jim Lewis, Valerie Lippincott,
Mary L. Lippold, Lenny Marvin, Grant Matthews, Maria Lyn
McGinnis, Tracy Medeiros, Karen Mouton, Natalie Ige
Muldaur, Mary Jo Niedzielski, John Niermann, Perry Patton,
Jerry Penacoli, Carolee Rhoades, Deirdre Richardson,
Jennifer Ruiz, Cork & Mary Rugroden, Roland Rutjens,
Don Scott, Nancy Sills, Cathy Smith, Art Spaeth,
Elaine Springer, Carl Timothy, Jesus Torres, Arthur Wayne,
Donald Wayne, Chuck J. Westmore, Barbara Wilcox,
Elliot Williams, Judith Wilson, Katie Wright, Greg Zarian and
anyone else who helped us in any way with this project.

Table of Contents

In my early days of vaudeville, my "favorite"

room was any backstage dressing space,

as long as it was inside the theatre. On Broadway,

it was my own dressing room with a private bathroom. Then I

married Dolores and everything changed, thank God! From our

first apartment in New York to our homes in Toluca Lake and

Palm Springs, Dolores not only created "favorite" rooms but she has

the talent to make something "favorite" in and about every room.

BOB HOPE

*T*he minute I saw this statue I fell in love with it. The title is Fatherhood, *and it represents*

a relationship that is at once both protective and liberating. I bought it as a potential gift for my

then boyfriend…having no idea I would

one day be giving it to him as an engage-

ment present. Much later, when I walked

into our desert home, I had an immediate

response to its natural beauty and strength.

Like the sculpture, there is a feeling of safety

and guardianship, yet a respect for the

necessity of freedom.

The sculpture fit perfectly in space and in

character. The decorating became rather

eclectic, with each room mixing old with new. It was all done from the standpoint of creating warmth

without suffocation, and comfort without regulation.

Brooke Shields

13

We feel that it's really important to make rooms look inviting. We want our family, friends, and guests to feel good about sitting down and staying awhile.

Our living room is a mix of both of us. Forest collects African art, so I put a lot of the pieces into this room. I added some floral fabrics on the pillows and ottomans to soften the room, and there are always a lot of fresh flowers and scented candles throughout our home.

I wanted the dining room to be intimate and cozy, so guests can have conversation over dinner. I had the table made with Forest in mind—being tall, I wanted him to feel comfortable while dining.

Forest bought me the beautiful vintage rocking horse after we were engaged.

I love it!

I decided to have a little fun on the staircase, hence the leopard!

Keisha & Forest Whitaker

When I first moved to Los Angeles, I had no house, no dog, no husband, and no sister. Ten years later, I have everything except a sister, but I've come to realize that this is my parents' responsibility.

My husband had been hiding, I mean residing, in a flat in London, and I had been flailing, I mean failing, in an apartment in New York City, so when we looked for the house of our dreams in California, the one thing we both craved was high

ceilings. As you will see when you turn the page, we have achieved our goal. Our living room ceiling is so high we were unable to include the top of it in the photograph. That's not a bad thing, because our ceiling is so high that it's impossible to clean—there is no apparatus that extends that far. Eventually we're going to have to cut a hole in the roof and dangle someone down wielding a damp cloth. But enough about our ceiling. Let's talk about our sofas.

Martin and I went shopping for sofas after we bought the house. We bought big sofas. We bought the biggest sofas on the market. They were not big enough. In fact nothing that we bought for this house was big enough because of those damn ceilings. We eventually enlisted the help of a talented woman who told us that everything we had bought was out of scale and would have to be "lacquered and put outside." We had an enormous coffee table fashioned out of an antique door that could have welcomed the Jolly Green Giant. The sofas can comfortably seat 72 and the aubisson (I have no idea how to spell this; I didn't live in France in the 19th century) that hangs over the fireplace is the longest in captivity.

As you can see, Martin and I like paintings that are totally out of touch with reality. We'd go into therapy and find out why, except that the paintings were so expensive, we can't afford it. Our entry hall has a painted ceiling that reminds me of the Caesars Palace Mall in Las Vegas. I usually walk in the front door and instinctively reach for my credit card. The Doberman that rests underneath the gigantic mirror is a sculpture that looks so real that our visitors pet it, then become so embarrassed, they no longer want to be our friend.

The bronze sculpture of a girl reading on the bench is a gift from my husband, who evidently wants me to read more. The dining room is where we eat all of our take-out food, and I'd show you the bedroom but it isn't done yet.

Rita Rudner & Bonkers

Ahoy mates, welcome aboard! Most people have their homes on solid ground, but our home floats on water. My husband, John, and I have lived on our 87-foot yacht for the past 10 years. He's owned several boats since he was 25 years old and knows everything about boating. The perfect captain, husband, and sailing mate, I might add!

On the main floor are the living room, dining room, kitchen, galley, desk for working, and a piano so I can rehearse my songs when needed. Up front on the same level is the command bridge, complete with a large table and built-in bench. In the rear of the boat is an outside deck with a long table and chairs for eating.

On the lower-level aft is the master suite with full bath and spa tub for me, and a full separate bathroom for John. Forward is an additional bedroom with a queen-size bed, full bathroom, and crew quarters with bunks that sleep four. Nearby is a workout room with a treadmill and a stair climber. Adjacent is the engine room that John keeps so immaculate you can eat off the engines!

On the upper deck is a large table with bench seating, bar, television, and a barbecue—all perfect for entertaining and watching the sights. You can steer the boat from the upper deck. Sometimes you'll even catch me behind the wheel!

Over the years we've made many trips, from Mexico all the way to the Caribbean. We love the fact that we never have to pack, we just take our home with us. Because of my hectic and fast-paced schedule, coming home to the water is the one way I can truly relax. Nothing better than to sit back at the end of a busy day and watch a beautiful sunset.

Florence Henderson

*H*aving been born under the astrological sign of Cancer, my home is a vital part of my life. I would like to think that it reflects at least a part of my personality. It is nestled on the top of a mountain in the Hollywood Hills, and it's called Villa des Lapins (House of Rabbits), for a very good reason. No, I didn't have some wild childhood nightmare about the Easter bunny. Actually, my former home back East plays a role in this story.

It was called The Briarpatch, so named by its previous owner who had collected years and years of beautiful antique rabbits. One was a priceless carousel head, which you see on this page. When I bought the house, these rabbits were inhabiting the attic. I feared the former owner had just forgotten them, but she reassured me that the rabbits stayed with the house. A friend of mine wrote a children's book about The Briarpatch, and rabbits became a fun collectible and a part of my home.

I moved West and bought this house, and the first morning I awoke in my little piece of paradise, I noticed the wildlife in the hills—and, you guessed it, a family of real rabbits was happily residing in my backyard. Since my house has a Mediterranean feel and reminds me of the south of France, it had to be named Villa des Lapins.

My home, inside and out, is filled with art and pieces of furniture that mean something to me—sculptures like *Boys on the Bridge, which, every time I look at it, makes me feel like a kid again.* The *Bronze Lady* stands watch by the simple Mediterranean-style pool (complete with mosaic mermaid), but turns her back to the city and canyon views, so as not to be upstaged.

When I sit at my piano, with my dog Jesse by my feet, and take in the magnificent views, I am reminded of how lucky I am to be working in the exciting world of showbiz in Hollywood, and to be able to live in a peaceful and serene environment right above all that excitement.

Jerry Penacoli & Jesse

The sparkling reflections on the water, the rustling of lush green trees, the fragrant and ever-shifting aroma of roses in the air, the joyous sound of splashing water, giggles, and laughter rising upward and floating around us, this is our garden…our special "room"…our heavenly haven.

When I found our home 12 years ago, there was much repair to be done but the bones were refined and excellent. The house is a handsome English Tudor, built in 1947 with fine details; the original owner was also a talented and avid gardener. She planted hundreds of exquisite rose bushes (we now have 400), and some of the bud unions (the bases) are so broad they rival young trees. She also planted a variety of specimen trees such as Aleppo pines, Arbutus unedo (strawberry tree), olives, and various fruit trees such as pomegranate, apple, plum, peach, and lemon.

I have added to this bounty over the years; one of my little treasures is a Tabebuia ipe (pink flowering trumpet tree). Flowers such as New Zealand rock lilies, yellow angels' trumpet, sage, lavender, ginger, kangaroo paws, Dichorisandra, orchids, tulips, poppies, and aromatic vines delight the senses. I have watched as each new addition grows along with our young boys.

Two years ago I transformed the original pool from its aged and well-worn condition into a colorful, whimsical, and exotic painting of glass mosaics surrounding three-dimensional, hand-carved animal-motif tiles. The bottom is finished with a smooth background of blue and gray pebbletech that blends to the edges of a contented moon, golden stars, and an enormous and alluring all-knowing eye. The children's favorite is the warm and relaxing spa, which also has glass tile inlays. Mathematically the oval pool layout with its elevation changes was quite a design challenge. I was constantly adjusting the patterns until I realized the most attractive and workable equation. My husband

and the children were somewhat less patient in the yearlong process, not quite sharing in my grand vision… they just wanted water! The new pool was a "gift" to my husband and the boys; it is where they spend the most time together. Wolf likes to come home between lunch and dinner at the restaurants and swim and play with them. They enjoy throwing lemons to Plato, our golden retriever, who dives, swims, and fetches them for hours.

Folksy, handmade windmills, elegant and unusual fountains of stone and bronze, and overflowing flower beds abound in our garden. Cameron and Byron delight in their cow on the roof that surveys all, and they never tire of running around in the secluded areas of their own "secret garden." The llamas, tortoises, birds, bunnies, cats, dogs, and lizards keep us all busy and amused. We are a large and eclectic family of God's creatures; ah, now, if we could just find a little more time to enjoy it all.

Barbara Lazaroff, Wolfgang Puck, Cameron, Byron & Plato

SHAMBALA

Whenever I return from Los Angeles, New York, or more exotic cities like Paris or Rome, or even my local community of Acton, California, I always feel my heart beat a little faster as I approach this magical place called The Shambala Preserve.

I have lived here since 1976. My rambling haven is of African decor; leopard and tiger prints abound (faux of course). I believe some of the most beautiful designs in the world are worn by the wildcats.

I am surrounded by magnificent felines. Jaffra, a Bengal tigress, sleeps and plays outside my guest bedroom. Daisey, a mountain lion, peers into my kitchen window. Ozzie and Sphinx, two African servals, dwell off my back deck. Lions and tigers live in a large compound in front of my home. Down the Santa Clara River on the 60-acre preserve reside leopards, lions, tigers, a cheetah, and across the lake, two of my biggest pals, our African elephants, Timbo and Kura.

One of my favorite rooms I call the tree room, which provides a perfect resting area and scratching post for the six sibling domestic kittens I've adopted. African artifacts adorn tabletops and walls. The two African shields on either side of the French doors once hung in William Holden's home in Palm Springs.

The fireplace room is a sanctuary, holding things I love, many from my daughter Melanie Griffith, mementos from my travels around the world and photos of the wild ones. It extends off my bedroom, which is warm, inviting, and a place in which photos of my family and friends along with set stills and posters of films I've done—precious reminders of special times—are pleasing sights on walls, dressers, and tabletops.

My dressing room became my own boutique organized by activity: Shambala clothes, city clothes, and evening dress. The body form was made to my exact measurements in the wardrobe department at Universal Studios when Edith Head designed my costumes for The Birds *and* Marnie. *I still use it!*

The hammock on the front deck is reserved for special moments, watching the lions and tigers sunbathe while listening to their roars and the elephants trumpeting. These things are indelibly imprinted in my mind.

My home, my haven, in the Sanskrit meaning of the word, Shambala, is truly a meeting place of peace and harmony for all beings, animal and human.

Tippi Hedren & Garth

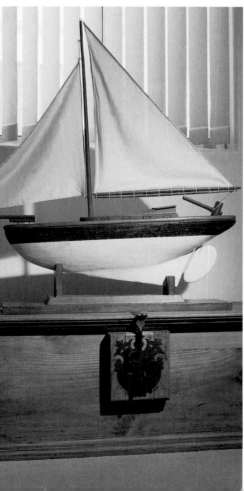

*M*y home is my sanctuary, the one place I can go to escape all the rigors of my

daily grind. For me it's very important that my house is also my home, and it's the

smallest of details that make mine special. While growing up in my parents' house, my mother always decorated

with elephants, because they are

said to bring their keepers good

luck. So in keeping with Cibrian

family tradition, I too incorporated

elephants into my decorating

process. I must say, so far my luck's

been pretty good.

I chose the living room as my

favorite room in the house because

of all the time and thought I've poured into it. I love the look of antique pine, cast iron, and traditional style thrown

into one. I find it's very comforting to have lots of pictures of loved ones and special times in my life around to

remind me how lucky I really am. Of course Wyatt, my Jack Russell terrier, is also a big part of my life. No room

would ever be complete without him roaming around ruling over his domain.

So for now I live with my beautiful

girlfriend Brandi, Wyatt, and the latest

addition to our family, an all original

vintage 1960 Chevrolet Corvette.

Eddie Cibrian & Wyatt

F·O·N·T·A·N·E

F·O·N·T·A·N·E·L

My husband, Ken Dudney, and I named our place FONTANEL, which means "the soft spot in a baby's head." We deemed this name appropriate because, during the designing phase, we did most everything with our children in mind—the log playground, indoor pool with hot tub, barbecue and kitchen, and a soda fountain room with pool table, game machines, jukebox, and small dance floor. We also have a television room with a 6- by 8-foot screen. Ken and I enjoy our "Great Room;" we call it that because we think it's great that we have it. It's 48 feet by 48 feet and is fabulous for entertaining. The dining room, my favorite room, seats 18 and is perfect for formal dinners with friends and family. Our 13 bathrooms and six bedrooms are designed for everyone's comfort. We spend most of our time in our family room, where we watch television, sit by the fireplace, and do most of our dining. A wonderful 300-gallon saltwater aquarium helps to soothe the hassles of everyday life.

Our land includes 141 acres of wooded hillside with some creek-bottom land seeded in grass, and the home sits at the end of a milelong drive at the back of a wooded valley. Ken has a Hughes 500D helicopter sitting on the helo-pad in the backyard for our enjoyment as well as for business.

When you arrive, we say, "Welcome to the wild kingdom," as we have about 30 feeders for the birds, squirrels, raccoons, deer, and turkeys. Our pets include a yellow lab, a bouvier, a cockatoo, two diamond doves, four cats, and a new Bengal cat kitten named Cheetah's Den Tsunami Kumate'.

Animals have always played a big part in our lives, so when Gunther Gebel-Williams, of Ringling Bros.

Barnum & Bailey circus, gave us "Sibra," one of his tiger skins, as a gift, we were absolutely thrilled. Gunther couldn't stand to bury his animals when they died, so he had them preserved for eternity. He had never before given one away until he gave this one to us. We are very proud to display it on the wall in our "Great Room," along with pictures of Gunther performing with Sibra.

Goldilocks loved the three bears and we do too, so we followed that theme, as they represent our three children, Matthew, Jaime, and Nathan. FONTANEL was truly built with love.

Barbara Mandrell & Tsunami Kumate'

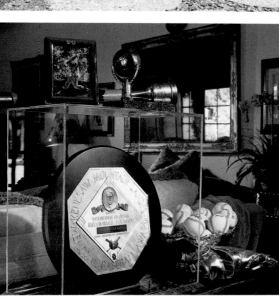

It all starts at the front door. Living behind gates made it possible to do something not only open, but unusual. A Dutch door seemed to be low-key and inviting. We wanted our guests to feel as though they were a part of our house, even before they rang the bell. Instead of having a carpenter make our door, I went to my favorite store in the world, Home Depot. The key was to hire a wonderful faux artist and put on pewter hardware from France. Finishing touches are everything.

"Everything we need or want is in our own backyard." That's the Garvey family motto. When we bought our own home it needed everything redone. A gardener hadn't graced its presence in over five years! Because the outdoors is our preferred space, we started there. It took us 18 months to manicure just under two acres, and, some 400 white iceberg roses later, this is what we created.

Buying antiques is my passion, and sitting in handmade leather chairs with memorabilia around is Steve's. These were the ideas I had in mind when creating Steve's space. The biblioteque is early 18th century Louis XV from the Loire valley, in the south of France. The antique table between the two leather chairs is one of my favorite pieces. Rich in birch wood, it's unmistakably a Biedermeier. Collecting one's own memorabilia is definitely more important to our children than to Steve. Steve did pick his most prized awards, however. The large plaque in Plexiglas is his favorite—the Lou Gehrig award. We also display a gold ball for his 1,100th RBI (Padres vs. Chicago, 1984); a framed copy of an original LeRoy Neiman of Steve; an Olympic torch from 1984; one of four Golden Gloves from 1984 for best first baseman; and a collection of autographed baseballs, from Babe Ruth to Cal Ripken.

Our master bedroom is my favorite room in the house. It's not a large retreat but warm, intimate, and very romantic when all the candles are lit. We chose an eastern king bed because we seem to never be without our two smaller children wanting to cuddle. The colors we chose are predominantly cream with accents of taupe and sage green. Every room in the house contains something of emotional value. The master suite is no different: Hanging over the antique tin and beveled mirror is my wedding veil.

What's next for the Garveys? Decorating the new baby's room.

Steve & Candace Garvey

*My home is a bit odd in that there is only one piece of furniture in my "Living Room."
The walls of this room are filled with art. My favorite pieces are a portrait that
John Mellencamp painted called* The Reverend Jim; *three screen credit cards from a*

*silent movie, which I found under my last
house in Hollywood; and a sketch drawing by
John Lennon of his family. With the elaborately
carved antique doors from Mexico, magnificent stone fireplace, and high-beamed ceilings,
it just seemed like "putting a bow on a
gilded cage" to put anything else in this room.
This is where I go to be alone (well, with my
fur family) and read.*

*Everyone always gathers in the kitchen/den
area, anyway, and in there I have lots of
places for everyone to hang out. I grow my
own herbs, which I have in pots right outside
the kitchen's French doors. I love to cook,
which is good because my friends love to eat.
The floor tiles were handmade in Mexico, so
the dog prints are not the only prints you will
find here. Birds and cats and who knows
what else also made their way across my tiles
before they were dry. The dining room is great
for formal or informal meals with its large*

*French doors that look out onto a side patio. This room I did very simply also, except for the leopard print on the chair
seats, because I want the focus to be on the people in the room, not the room itself.*

*This house has a lot of surprises: the paw prints in the tile flooring, the water fountain hidden in the bushes outside,
and the two doves that return here every year to build a nest and raise their
family in my grapefruit tree.*

*I am definitely a nester. "At home" is my favorite feeling and my
favorite place to be!*

Kay Lenz, Billie & Pony

*W*hen my first child was born, I bought my own Fifth-Wheel Dressing Room.

Though I was working, I nursed my children for

several years. They were always with me. I bought it for them

to have continuity in their lives, as a home away from home—

their bed, their pictures on the walls, their bathtub, and their

toys in the cupboards. That was two boys and 15 years ago. Our

big, old, 40-foot, Fifth-Wheel Pop-Out put in her time.

Now, since my children are older and don't spend all their time

with me anymore, I decided to get a smaller self-contained

motor home—one I can drive—and it's decorated for me. All the fabrics are natural fiber. This one's for

work and play. I love it, and the kids love

it. It's our rain forest on wheels.

Lindsay Wagner

*W*e knew we were home the minute we heard the rushing of the waterfall! It's background music to the squeals from our two children, who can't wait to go outside every day and discover what new magic the seasons have brought to our doorstep. We live in a town only "45 minutes from Broadway" as the song goes, yet worlds away from the bustle of the big city. Our home started its life as a Dutch farmhouse in the mid 1800s, with a working sawmill on the land and ancient Indian caves from the Lenape tribe dotted along the length of the river that runs through the property. A dam was built with a massive waterwheel to power the machinery, and the remains of those structures still exist on the land, adding a true sense of history to the already evident peace and calm of the rushing water and acres of forest surrounding us.

We needed a clean and especially inspiring environment to raise the kids and do our real work besides show business—creating pottery. We chose a house that had a lineage of creative souls, having been in the playwright Maxwell Anderson's family for over 75 years. Rebuilt in 1924 by Anderson and a well-known artist and woodcarver, Carroll French, it stands today still intact, with all the evocative interior touches like carved balustrades and beams out of local chestnut to represent all the indigenous plants and animals. Above the front door as you leave, the latin phrase Exeuntomnes is etched, which means "all go out" or, simply put, EXIT! Anderson worked on What Price Glory?, Saturday's Children, and subsequent works in the attic study overlooking the waterfall. The only new construction we've done so far is to convert an old garage/chicken coop into a light and warm work space for our pottery. Working in entertainment, we are blessed with a lifestyle that not only feeds our hungry growing family but also keeps us intimately in touch with the elements of life—earth, fire, and water!

Barry & Sherri Ellen Bostwick

Moi's home is like moiself—fantastique, romantique, and expensive. The petit powder room arrayed here before vous is the type one might find aboard that legendary ship featured in last year's big boat movie. (When I wish to relive my favorite moment from that movie, I come to this room and shout at the top of my lungs: "Moi is Queen of the World!")

As vous can see, the room has been subtly decorated in a style meant to suggest the glory days of the Medicis, the Borgias, and the Spellings. Every appointment is awash in ornamental frippery, thus creating a frisson of exquisite effervescence that is sure to please. (Hey, that's what the decorator said.)

Here, I can escape the pressures of being internationally fabulous and enjoy the simple pleasures granted those of us who make so much by doing so little for so many.

Here, amidst the best and most of everything, moi can dream a dream, savor a chocolate, write a love poem, savor a few more chocolates, sip a little bubbly, savor the second level of chocolates, contemplate the beauty of a rose or a jewelry catalogue, and wonder why there aren't any more chocolates to savor.

Here, surrounded by a level of luxury that is sure to inspire fits of jealousy from everyone else in this book, I am at peace with moiself and moi's stuff.

Here, where moi can truly be moi, I am sheltered by elegance, enraptured in romance, and wrapped in the warm embrace of a bubble bath… or an amphibian.

Hard to believe this place is a sublet.

Miss Piggy

*I*f the home is a sanctuary, then the heart of my sanctuary is my bedroom!

When Sonny and I first lived together, we only had so much money. We went downtown to the secondhand shops and bought just enough furniture to strip, sand, and refinish in order to fill our bedroom. Therefore, we slept, ate, played gin, and watched television in that bedroom.

In our living room, we had an old upright piano that Son said "was a bargain at $85, because it only had three broken keys." We also had a square dining table that Son worked on for so long that he whittled it down to a very low coffee table, which, in the end, he stained blue.

This was the beginning of a pattern. My bedrooms since then have gotten progressively larger, which suits me just fine.

Cher

The gym and beautiful, expansive grounds are two main reasons why we bought this house.

We entertain frequently and the yard can accommodate just about anything! From casual barbecues to

formal receptions, our backyard, with its heavenly views

(especially at the sunset hour), makes everyone feel welcome,

cozy, and comfortable without being ostentatious. Our

watchful bear was a gift from our good friends Randy and

Heather Hill. At first glance, most people think our gym is a

guest house. It actually was built as a gym by the former

owner. As my husband, Edward, and I work out with our

trainer three mornings a week (at 5:30 A.M.!), we really appreciate

the luxury of not having to drive to a gym. I watch my I Love

Lucy *videos while being tortured on the treadmill; it sure makes*

the time pass faster when I'm laughing! Edward decided he would set up his beloved

train set (always a work in progress!) in one corner. This way we can work

hard and have fun at the same time. We also use the gym for much needed

massages and saunas.

Melody Thomas Scott

We had moved out of our house and were living temporarily in an apartment while searching for our dream home. It was December and I had come back from performing Sweet Charity on Broadway. My husband, Norman Nixon, picked me up for lunch one day and we headed out to Santa Monica. However, we didn't end up at a restaurant. He drove into this neighborhood with wide streets and tall palm trees and pulled up in front of this house—a house that was overgrown like Sleeping Beauty's castle, with bushes and trees at least 12 feet high. You couldn't even see the house from the sidewalk! Norman led me up to these iron gates. I looked at him and said "What is this?" He answered, "This might be our new house if you like it." We walked in, and there we saw this beautiful, big white house with a shingle roof. It had magnificent, tall, double antique oak front doors. We walked in, and, for me, it became even more amazing. There was this long two-story hallway with a wood staircase; it felt like a gallery space. It had dark wood floors and dark chocolate carpeting in the living room along with an antique fireplace. When we got to the end of the hallway, I turned to the left and saw this huge kitchen. This was the kitchen of all times, the kind I had always dreamed about having one day. It had wonderful wood floors, tall counters, beautiful cabinets, a skylight, and a big, big picture window that looked out over the back. I just sat there on the brick fireplace hearth in awe and got so excited that I said "Yes! Yes!" and started jumping in Norman's arms. I hadn't even seen the rest of the house.

As we continued walking through, it kept unfolding more and more surprises. It was like a great movie that just kept building and building. It had three bedrooms upstairs that were perfect for children. One was like a doll's house, ideal for my 2-year-old, Vivian. I was pregnant at the time with our second child. Outside it had a lap pool, a tennis court, and a big guest house. This was the home for us!

Before moving in we made a lot of changes. I stripped all the dark stain from the floors and woodwork and restored them to their natural color, and replaced the dark carpeting in the living room with bleached white oak floors. I made new marble fireplaces everywhere. I wanted the rooms open and bright. I never hired an interior decorator; we wanted to do it ourselves. I designed everything with Norman and the children in mind. The gallery entry was perfect for our art that we love so much. The kitchen is the big meeting place for everyone. There's always lots of activity— chatting, reading, watching television, doing homework, cooking, and eating; it's like "cafe central." Norman surprised me one day and designed a dance studio right off my dressing room with a high, churchlike ceiling.

Over the years we've collected some wonderful pieces of art from many different artists. Ed Dwight gave Norman his incredible sculpture of strong hands reaching up manipulating a basketball. I always thought it would make a great logo for the NBA. It's the centerpiece in the entry. One of my favorite pieces of art was done by one of the most renowned sculpturists of today, Tina Allen. It's an impression of Judith Jamison. It spoke to me so personally, about who we are, how we live our lives, and what our work and joys are.

Our house is a "family house," open to all our family and friends to enjoy. I was very lucky to have a husband who had such great taste and instincts on how we wanted to live. This is truly our little niche of heaven.

Debbie Allen

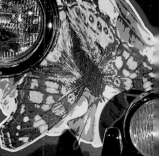

f the amount of pleasure one receives from a certain space is any indication of the amount of time

one spends in that place, my favorite spot would have to be my studio. Occupying two industrial buildings

near the ocean in Malibu, this is where many of my dreams are realized. Including offices and several expansive areas,

the studio is where I can escape to do what I like to do: work.

The studio is where my ideas for projects gestate and grow. And until these

projects are ready to be exhibited to the public, I am able to freely indulge in

the environments that they activate. A part of the studio houses up to 20

Mercedes Benz 220A cabriolets from my series, Earthly Paradise, *when they are*

not traveling in exhibitions worldwide. The studio is also one of the places

where I was able to experiment with the effects of holographic mylar and lasers

for my installation titled Element. *Whether working on a new series of*

photographs or actualizing my next project, the studio represents for me the

gratification of home.

Hiro Yamagata

This acre of land overlooking the Pacific Ocean was transformed into an art studio and multipurpose recreational area. The pool area has a solar-heated lap pool, spa, wading pool, and a deep diving pool. The diving pool bottom is tiled with a school of sharks. When the water stirs, the illusion of them swimming is quite complete. Helicopters have been known to circle overhead to view this 007 scenario. The stand of blue concrete palm trees is built of rebar wrapped around railroad ties, which are buried four feet in the ground to support the upper weight of the concrete fronds. The first set snapped in half in the 100 mph ocean breeze, but this fiberglass–reinforced set has survived the worst of El Niño. On a clear day the blue concrete pool blends perfectly with the sea and sky. Ah, life on the edge…

The studio itself is designed with 40-foot ceilings with gymnastic rings; nine-foot double doors enable extremely large paintings to pass through with ease. The four-foot clerestory windows along the spine of the roof ensure a steady northern light. The loft area, originally intended as a clean graphic area, mutated into a very plush master suite with whale watching for your toothbrushing pleasure.

The well-thought-out kitchen, which started its life as a darkroom, is extremely efficient and loaded with storage. Its dark wood craftsman interior contrasts nicely with custom sheet-metal detailing.

The large shower/sauna area is a combination of different-

sized glass blocks utilizing the wonderful privacy and light qualities of the material without the boring repetition usually seen. The unusual design of the tile work was accomplished by laying out millions of small pieces of paper in endless combinations to find the perfect combination of tile and glass. Tiling the sauna door streamlined the wall. The antique pedestal sink and art nouveau armoire balance the crisp tile design, making a very user-friendly place whose door leads us back to the pool area. Not a bad place to be.

Cheech Marin

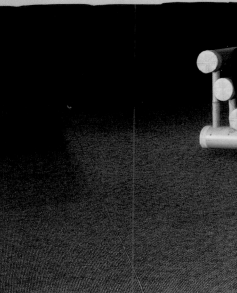

Schatzi
ON MAIN

*I*n designing Schatzi on Main, our primary goal was to offer gemuetlichkeit, *which*

refers to a warm and comfortable atmosphere. We tried to keep it simple and clean, so

that the look of the restaurant was second only to the food. The

lush, covered outdoor patio was included to be reminiscent of the

many outdoor cafes and restaurants found throughout Austria

and Germany as well as to offer an area for our monthly cigar-

night event.

We have displayed some of our favorite artwork from Anthony

Quinn and Hiro Yamagata, and even a drawing done by

myself! The beautifully scalloped brick ceiling, copper fixtures,

and terra-cotta planters all lend to the warm and friendly

atmosphere that Maria, international designer Adam Tihany,

and I were striving to achieve. Maria added the artistic flower arrangements and is responsible for hand-

picking the china, among other things.

Stopping in at Schatzi on Main always takes me back home.

Arnold Schwarzenegger

y office, where I spend a great deal of my time, is a space I've tried to make as comfortable as my home. The wonderful antique door, with etched glass, opens into the entry, where we have a bench to rest from the fast-orbiting world. From the entry you descend down several steps into a sitting area with comfy couches and chairs—a fine spot to relax with friends and visitors, read, or catch a quick nap. The area with my desk, which surrounds me on three sides, is filled to the brim with things I've received or collected over a lifetime. The problem now is I've really outgrown this space and can't find any more room to put things. Half the time I can't find what I'm searching for, but thankfully my beautiful wife, Lois, always seems to know just where to find it. I love my West Point chair because it has wheels on it and I can roll to where I need to go around my desk. Some of my favorite items include my 1951 West Point graduation arm band, Apollo 11 patch, Lunar Lander replica, Presidential Medal of Freedom, U.S. Astronaut Hall of Fame Medal, Bottom Gun cap given to me by the man who initially

located the sunken Titanic, *and one of my best friends, Buzz Lightyear. There is also a picture and a replica of a Vega Red Eagle airplane that I took my first ride in at age two. The dramatically high ceilings throughout the different areas give an open feeling. From any point around the office you can always look out the big picture windows and see a spectacular ocean view. Because I travel a great deal for business, I always look forward to coming home and spending time in my office. It's a very relaxing and comfortable atmosphere. When I make that first step into this room, surrounded by a lifetime of memories, I always reflect back to that one moment when I put that first step onto the Moon…and that was just the beginning!*

Buzz & Lois Aldrin

U.S. ASTRONAUT HALL OF FAME®

BUZZ ALDRIN
March 20, 1993

BOTTOM
GUN

1951

*M*y house was built in 1926, in a neighborhood now designated as a historical

preservation zone. I stumbled across the house two years ago and saw

its potential immediately. It had all its original period features intact, including a speaking tube connecting the

upstairs landing to just outside the
front door, which works remarkably
well as a primitive intercom system.
All the objects in the house have
been accumulated over the eight
years I've lived in California, so
I had no idea how any of it would
work in this home. To my delight,
I found it incredibly easy. The
house is very warm and friendly,
and the garden a sort of eccentric

English mess. I'm constantly delighted by how fast my plants and trees grow here in the California sunshine, a far

cry from the long winter months I endured growing up in London. My parents are antique dealers, and looking

at my eclectic choice of furnishings, it seems I too have the collectors

bug. My dog, Sir William, was born in Topanga Canyon and

rescued from a remote location where I was filming. He's actually

named after the character Bruce Dern played in the movie Billy,

but his full titles are Sir William of Dog, Sir William, or,

simply, William of Dog.

Amanda Donohoe & Sir William of Dog

Milton Berle
Dean Martin
Mary Livingstone
George Burns
GRACIE ALLE

Our garden in our Beverly Hills home is one of our favorite spots. It has a walkway with signed names of many of our famous friends who have visited us over the years. It's like strolling down memory lane. The path fills us with many happy and sad moments. Some of these friends are long gone, others still fill the silver screen.

We like works of art, and our garden is populated with them. Two pieces of sculpture are from William Holden's garden in Palm Springs. The others were bought at different times whenever we found something we liked. You can find us from time to time cleaning or polishing them.

On warm evenings we have dinner in our garden, and sometimes when we have a large group we cover the pool. All the sculptures are lit from the trees and they look like they belong there, because they know we enjoy them.

Kirk & Anne Douglas

The unique Roman-Grecian bathroom makes me feel a part of my heritage. After a long day, my wife and I enjoy relaxing together in the large Italian marble bathtub. The tub was carved in Italy, in one piece, from a block of marble belonging to Julius Caesar's own quarry. The designer did a larger duplicate of Caesar's own personal tub that adds a historical feel to the room and to our Mediterranean villa. The visual mood in my bathroom has the warm glow of a room of art.

The boudoir, as we like to call it here at the Honey Hill Estate, is my private space. I feel it is extremely important for everyone to have a space or room of their own, and I feel blessed that my space is such an extension of whom I try to be.

It is best described as romantic French with a dash of the South—yeehaw! It is cozy, warm, soft, and feminine in spirit. The craftsmanship that was put into creating

this room, from the beautiful inlaid marble floors to the incredible paintings of heavenly angels and roses to the romantic spa bathtub and open shower, makes me feel like a princess every time I enter it.

I truly adore my boudoir because this is where I spend many of my days in Malibu, napping with our new baby or having peaceful, intimate moments relaxing with my husband. As we lie here, its peace is very forgiving for our fast-paced lifestyle. This room is truly my dream space.

John Paul, Eloise &
John Anthony DeJoria

I have strong personal ties to Memphis, Tennessee. It holds special memories for me. The rich musical and cultural heritage, the down-home cooking, living at Graceland, and all the good times with Elvis. I've lived in California for a number of years and my life and my work have taken me around the world, but I always love going back to Memphis. In so many ways it still feels like home.

As chairman of the board and president of Elvis Presley Enterprises, the pleasure of going to Memphis is often combined with the work I do with our management team. One project that we're all so proud of is our restaurant, Elvis Presley's Memphis, which opened there on historic Beale Street in 1997.

Our staff and team of consultants started with Elvis' own colorful tastes and personality, his body of work, his musical interests and influences, his reputation of warmth and care toward his close friends and his public, his sense of fun, and his strong ties to his hometown. The building itself was once home to Lansky Brothers' men's store, where Elvis bought many of his cool clothes in the '50s, and where he and many of the greats of Memphis shopped for years. We wanted a place where people from all walks of life, all age groups, and all musical interests would feel comfortable and at home. In putting all these elements together, the idea was to create a restaurant and live entertainment venue that Elvis himself might have owned and enjoyed.

Elvis Presley's Memphis has a campy elegance to it, sort of a '90s twist on the style of Graceland. Subtly displayed are mementos from Elvis' career and personal life, along with items that celebrate the Memphis music and culture that influenced him so deeply. The food is upscale American cuisine with some down-home Southern favorites. The hospitality and service are first rate. Elvis music and video programming play intermittently. On stage, it's live music— rock, gospel, rhythm and blues, and even some country. It's the music that influenced Elvis and the music he influenced.

We named our VIP room The Eagle's Nest after one of the Memphis juke joints Elvis performed in at the start of his career. This is my personal haven within Elvis Presley's Memphis, just as it is for the celebrated musicians, dignitaries, and other special guests we entertain there. The piano is always in tune and ready to go, should an impromptu jam session break out. We wanted to capture the spirit of all those jam sessions Elvis and his friends enjoyed on the road, in the recording studio, in his Vegas suite, and in his music room at Graceland. The decor is sort of a "retro funk." The big hair I'm wearing in the photo with Elvis and Tom Jones fits right in, don't you think?

The neon sign incorporates a stack of gold records topped with a radio tower. To me it symbolizes the power and magic of Elvis and Memphis music that has been beamed throughout the world. The photograph of Elvis playing pool was made in Memphis at his home on Audubon Drive, where he lived just before moving into Graceland. He was a good shot, but I can remember him moving a ball or two around to his advantage, just to see if the guys would challenge his bending of the rules. The fabric-lined pool room gets its inspiration from Elvis' own pool room at Graceland. The table is from one of the homes we had in California. The Beatles enjoyed a few rounds on it when they came to visit Elvis in the mid-'60s. It was a truly historic moment in rock 'n' roll. The 1960 Gibson J-200 was one of Elvis' favorite guitars. He played it at home and on stage through the early '70s. The beautiful stained glass partition is an artistic interpretation of the famous Graceland gates. It separates the VIP room from the rest of the venue when we have special guests. Some of Elvis' stage and personal wardrobe and other items are part of the exhibits within the restaurant, all carefully encased with special lighting.

Everything about Elvis Presley's Memphis feels right. It has become a special haven for me when I'm in town, and I'm thrilled to see that it has become a haven for so many people from Memphis and from all over the world.

Priscilla Presley

ost of the furnishings for our living room and formal dining room area were picked out by my 14-year-old daughter, Chantale, and myself. It's one of our favorite areas because it is not only beautiful but warm and full of love as well. We entertain here frequently…Chantale tinkles on the piano while I sing. My sweetheart, Landrus, and I also love this area because it is very cozy and romantic when the fireplace is lit on cool nights.

I often say that our kitchen and family room area closely resemble Grand Central Station when company comes over. We don't mind it a bit because we're all very high energy and really love people. Landrus and I have a great passion for cooking, and I must admit that he knows his way around a kitchen almost as well as I do! This area is also where we have great times watching television and sports events.

Roses, I love roses! My gazebo has 19 different varieties. When in bloom, the scent is so relaxing and heavenly that it nearly puts you to sleep.

Aside from our deep love and devotion for each other, Landrus and I also share an enjoyment for art and music. I particularly like collecting instruments such as violins, guitars, and pianos.

We also like pottery and sculpture pieces. During one of our relaxing walks while on a romantic weekend trip to Sausalito, we discovered a new best friend depicted on a piece of Santa Clara pottery. His name is Kokopelli. He is a Hopi Indian symbol that brings peace, joy, hope, and contentment into our lives…and isn't that something we all deserve?

JoMarie Payton & Landrus S. Clark

My office and conference rooms reflect the focus of my career—creating characters for film. In the conference room, I am surrounded by the characters themselves,

a constant inspiration and reminder of what my work day is about. My office, too, has a character of its own. It's a space to be creative in. My drawing table and sculpting stand fit comfortably in the loft-like atmosphere. All the touches—from the warmth of the woods to the strength of granite, cold stainless steel, the glass, the fluid curves, hard edges, and soft corners—live together in harmony.

It's also a great place to kick back. There's a cappuccino bar, four custom humidors housing some of the world's finest cigars, and overstuffed leather cushions that invite you to flop, have a cigar, and read a script.

A great deal of creative energy went into the design of my office and I believe the ambiance that has evolved inspires the creative mind.

Stan Winston

It is our world filled to the edges with dreams and wonderful memories. Having traveled the world over, every painting, porcelain item, and artifact is a part of a giant jigsaw puzzle that, now completed, has formed a beautiful picture. Each piece has its own story to tell, from the 16th century to today.

More importantly, it becomes the story of our lives. I would love to say I have a favorite, or a funny story to tell about each piece, but strangely enough we have no favorites. Because each day, in a different mood, I can relate to another time in my life. Pictures of many friends—Nancy and Tina Sinatra, Mae West, Josephine Baker, Elton John, Kathie Lee Gifford, Teddy Getty, and Ivana Trump, among others—sit quietly on the piano and every table, reminding us of wonderful moments of our lives gone by.

Each painting seems to come to life and we, strange as it may sound, visit with the people in them and hear their stories. We are never alone. Music often fills the rooms. We have lived in such a way that when the door closes there is no world outside.

The wondrous part is sharing with friends the joys and pleasure of the different periods of art that bring some fantasy to their lives. Yes, our home, I am sure, would appear cluttered to many other people, but to us, it is our life. I cannot tell you more, because each picture is worth a thousand words. But being ageless antiques, I often wonder who will live and love them next. There is an old saying: "No one really owns anything, we live in a world filled with borrowed beauty."

Mr. Blackwell & R.L. Spencer

I count the minutes from when I leave the set of The Nanny and cross Santa Monica Boulevard until I reach my newly renovated home in Beverly Hills. Once it was Shirley Temple's house. She should see it now. It's so exciting; it's like falling in love. When my designer asked me what I wanted my house to look like, I said, "Like a movie star's house."

The minute I get home I walk through each new room and say, "I like this room the best. I love it, I love it, I love it! Yet, the next room I walk through, I feel the same way. It is true, I'm having a love affair with my house.

My peach kitchen is my favorite room. It's so peaceful after a busy day on the set. I remember the days searching for the perfect cupboards and how amazed I was when Michael Kienzl, at Bradco Kitchens, showed me the beautiful pearl peach cupboard styles and the latest built-in conveniences. Not one space is wasted—it's all so efficient. Great! Michael Allen—Nancy Jr. and Nancy Sinatra Sr.'s decorator— convinced me to use all Kitchen Aid appliances because they are stainless steel, stunning, and guaranteed for life. This gives me the space to make my kitchen a real sitting room as well as surround myself with all my fairies and angels, including a painting by Mark Bennet of Santa Barbara, who designed The Wedding of the Fairies on tile for me. He hand painted the faces from photos of my friends and family. I have my favorite table by my sofa serving grapes to me, of course. Terry Landeck, my designer, was adamant that there be no curtains. She tiled the back splash about the granite countertops with soft peach tiles and carried the tiles around the windows instead of curtains for the softness. This gives me a great view of the Italian gardens, wonderful daylight, and lots of window sills for my angels and fairies to surround me.

There's a secret door to the office that my husband, Joe Bologna, and I share. It's hidden by bookshelves and a bear coat rack I gave Joe as a gift when we received our Emmys for "Acts of Love—And Other

Comedies." Joe collects bears and elephants, especially the elephants that leave their trunks up, which signify good luck. He also keeps his first pair of cowboy boots there. I guess this means good luck also. This office really is my favorite room. It's so full of warm memories and so inspiring. We have such fun here writing together, fighting together, and making up together. Yes, this is my favorite room. It's just a few steps up to our bedroom from the office. After many hours of writing on our new play we hit the peach master suite. Oh, how I love this comfortable room. Joe watches the television and I look at my doll collection and play with my puppies, Phil and Angel. I slip into a marble bath filled with bubbles, inspired by Greer Garson's bathroom, which I saw on a tour of movie star homes. I look at all the angels and fairies surrounding the tub and look out the windows at the palm trees in my garden in the moonlight and contemplate whether or not I am like a movie star. Oh, yes, this really, really is my favorite room.

Renee Taylor & Joe Bologna

*Y*ou know how the Mormons believe you should have two years worth of food stored in case the end of the world arrives and somehow you live through it, but you have to eat? Or something like that.

Well, I have the exact same idea when it comes to my house, only it's not about storing two years worth of food—it's about having at least two years worth of mind-engaging objects on hand. For, you know, when it's the end of the world, somehow you'll be able to get food delivered, but you won't be able to leave the house. I make up this scenario in my head and then I decorate. Well, for starters I must have about a zillion books. I like to have a lot of books around that I have read, but also lots I haven't read. You know, for when Armageddon arrives and you just get sooooo bored and you need something to read. And that means I have to have a lot of art, and interesting colors on the walls, and tons of videos and laser discs and pictures.

So that's basically my decorating strategy: How much interesting stuff can I cram into a room, but still make it NOT seem crowded or messy? And how can the colors be just the ones that make you want to read? And, fulfilling all this, how can it be a peaceful, rejuvenating place?

I'm not sure if I've succeeded with these criteria. But I do know that I'm in love with my house. Sometimes I feel like my house is my lover and we need time alone together. Then there's other times when my house just isn't cooperating with me (electricity, getting that piece of furniture into the corner) and I feel like we should go to couples therapy.

When my brother was sick with cancer and staying with me, along with my parents, the living room became the center of everything. I have so many wonderful memories of him, lots of great meals, lots of just watching the tube. I tried to follow a color scheme closest to that of my grandmother, Henrietta Sweeney, who died almost 20 years ago. Her house was filled with dark colored walls and dark wood furniture. Your eyes were never bored looking around her home. It was comfortable, relaxed, pleasing to the eye, and you almost felt like you could sink into it. Fortunately I inherited her piano, several of her lamps, many paintings, and her china. When my sister visited me from Japan, she said, "The spirit of Grandma Sweeney is in your house." I treasure that comment and believe it's true.

Now my boyfriend, Carl, lives here with me. I was so glad my house was willing to let another person into our relationship—but my home is open-minded that way. I guess my house knows that my love for it isn't compromised by my love for Carl.

Julia Sweeney

*I*f it's true when they say "home is where the heart is," then those who may look for my heart needn't look further than behind the gates of this place I call "Parodias Hacienda," meaning "House of Paradise," so named because it truly is that to me.

When the time came for me to purchase a home for myself, the task of finding the perfect one turned out to be a much longer and more difficult process than I'd ever imagined. My steadfast insistence on finding the home that would not only appeal to my eyes, but touch my heart and soul as well, turned what would've been a simple, ordinary process into an arduous and time-consuming task that ended after two years of constant "look-sees" and open walk-throughs. But I must say it was worth every minute I spent searching. Upon first sight of this place, it took about 20 seconds for me to realize that I had finally found the place where my heart would be at peace and my soul would be satisfied.

When I had to decide which room was my favorite, it was impossible for me to pick one, because my house as a whole is what I love most about it. I chose the backyard because it's the part of the home that my family and friends seem to enjoy the most. The moment one steps into the area, the sound of the huge waterfall, which I had built into the side of the mountain surrounding the property, is the first thing one notices, and almost immediately provides a soothing sense of calm. The fact that its warm waters flow gently down into a large hot tub and spa might add to its pleasurable appeal. Alongside it is the large, kidney-shaped pool that steps up into a canvas domed workout room, which houses a working antique jukebox, large-screen color television, and VCR. One of my favorite areas of the backyard is the canvas-draped tree house that overlooks the entire yard. Since it sits so high, I thought it was the perfect area to house my telescope, which I use to watch my neighbors, oops, I mean the stars. Toward the back of the yard are two guest houses that each have a different theme. The first is reminiscent of the inside of a pirate ship, and is designed to resemble the captain's quarters, because if I owned a pirate ship I would most definitely have to be nothing less than the captain of it. The second guest house is reminiscent of an Old West cabin, and it's sort of my personal tribute to those brave pioneers who had to suffer the hardships of no hot running water and no electricity. The house I had built has both—I'm nostalgic, not crazy.

Reginald VelJohnson & Brutus

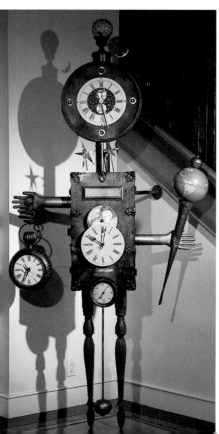

*T*hat song that Julie Andrews made so famous, "These Are a Few of My

Favorite Things," certainly describes my room. All of the things that I love dearly somehow

found their way into a place I call my

office. As you can see, it is a great deal

more than that.

There is a representation

of the blues; I love to sing

the blues. There is a clown;

I love clowns! And of course my overhead trains, which

actually run, will liven up any business meeting!

There are airplanes, because I flew in World War II and

Korea and my favorite plane was the Corsair. I was a

Marine fighter pilot! And, of course, my life's work has to

be strongly represented in broadcasting. There is a

replica of my first microphone. It was used to announce

a bingo game, but as far as I was concerned, it represents

the great artistry of Jack Benny. Nearby, just outside the doors, is my clock. Being a broadcaster and a Marine, I am

a stickler for being on time.

Someone interviewing me once asked me what I wanted on my tombstone. I don't plan to have a tombstone, if I

have anything to do with it, but if I did the message would be: He was a good broadcaster and a great Marine.

And then there is my favorite thing, my lovely wife, Pam. She joins me often

in my room at meal times, for a meeting, or just to chit chat

and catch up.

What else in the world could a man wish for?

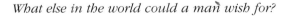

Ed & Pam McMahon

*I*t was love at first sight. I lust for wood, and I have to have light. This was the house for me.

Built by Harwell Hamilton Harris, a protégée of Frank Lloyd Wright's, my home has clean lines, light

for days, and a spiritual quality that all who visit it remark

upon. There are no compartments, no divisions; it flows.

I'm not a pool person, but there it was: the predictable aqua

California swimming pool with the brick patio. Something

had to be done. Too many months and too many dollars later,

there wasn't a brick to be seen…just a sea of adequin, slate,

and a beautiful blue-gray lagoonlike pond with two sexy water-

falls. I could watch them all day.

My father was a hero, the most decorated Air Force pilot of

World War II. He flew a B-17 called "The Swoose." It now lives

in the Smithsonian Air and Space Museum and I'm busy

trying to live up to the name. As a child, I yearned to be Mary or

Jane, but now I'm thankful for a name that serves me well in

my profession—they may mispronounce it, they may misspell it,

but they don't forget it.

Swoosie Kurtz

My office is the answer to the question: "What to do with the circular space at the base of an 84-foot hat?" The "hat" is the centerpiece of Robert Stern's design for The Walt Disney Company's Feature Animation Building. It duplicates in rather a large fashion the famous Sorcerer's Hat worn by Mickey Mouse in Fantasia. *Viewed from the exterior, it is a wonderful, pragmatic statement of what the building is all about. On the inside, it is potentially a wasted space, especially for the artists who work in the building. There is no natural light, there is nowhere to put an animator's desk, and, since the walls all lean in, there is no place to hang a storyboard. So, I volunteered to make use of what is, in effect, the inside of a giant cone. I'm glad I did.*

Some wonderful furniture was designed—to make use of the room's unique dimensions—that made me quickly feel right at home. I was left with only three problems: First of all, without any corners to anchor their spacial expectations, some visitors would literally get dizzy just sitting in the room. So, I hung a lot of pictures, and they seem to have calmed down people's inner ears. Second, there are remarkable acoustics inside Mickey's hat, making for some unexpected echoes on occasion. Third, there's the problem of the glass doors that lead into the room. They make for a nearly constant audience of people walking by and staring in. But, I can't blame them. In this age of cookie-cutter office spaces, it's not every day that one gets to see a truly "Fantastic" office. What's more, there's something to be said for a room that invariably puts a smile on the face of anyone who peers in through those glass doors—and on mine, as well.

Roy Disney

*P*eople see this beautiful view for the first time when they enter through the front door into the foyer. I love a lot of natural light. I wanted to keep a sense of openness in the hallway. I found the leather armchair at a shop in Fremont, Nebraska, and the pine table in Sonoma. The side table came from New Orleans. The off-white entry leads to my sienna-colored dining room. The colors of Italy, specifically Tuscany, are spread throughout my home.

The kitchen has to be my favorite room in the house. Everyone always seems to congregate there. I wanted to keep away from being overly formal, so I decided on a country-style kitchen. It has a homey feeling that's casual and inviting. The stove is the only part of the kitchen that remains from the original structure, and everything else was designed around it. The floors were given an antique look by putting black lines in between the wide pine boards. I wanted the floor to have a lived-in look, so the contractor and his crew distressed the boards by walking on them after spilling boxes of nails and screws.

The television room is where I spend most of my time, and is by far the most used area of my home. It's a cozy space where I can entertain and order Chinese food with friends. The two chairs are perfect for napping. This is the room where I choose the music that I skate to. I have a walk-in closet that houses a collection of about 2,000 CDs spanning every imaginable type of music.

When I'm up on the deck, I feel like I'm on top of the world. There is no better place to have a barbecue or absorb the spectacular view. I start every morning up on the deck with a mug of coffee and the morning paper. Most mornings I can hear a seal barking from nearby Pier 39.

Brian Boitano

115

*A*mbassadors for our ocean animals everywhere, Baby Shamu and I leap out of the water at Sea World's

Shamu Stadium, showcasing our power and strength and also letting thousands of park guests learn

about the behavior of killer whales in the wild.

The shows at Shamu Stadium help park guests learn about the ocean

environment and how to conserve it for future generations.

Visitors who come face-to-face with us at Sea World often experience a

powerful connection to marine life. Many realize a new and

profound respect for marine animals, and become active in preserving

our native habitats.

Shamu & Baby Shamu

he one spot? My bedroom. When I'm happy or sad, dreamy, creative, sexy or

not, relaxed, tense, in love or not, that's where I hide. I feel protected, I don't know

why. Maybe it's the fire by the

pool maintaining the right

mood; or the candles in each

corner keeping "that" energy

alive. I grab my guitar,

painted for me as an angel by

an artist friend of mine,

Sergio Arau, and play all the

time. I write and sing, laugh

and cry, listen

to music, watch movies or television, talk on the phone—business or pleasure.

On my bed, I feel like I'm in the jungle, covered by branches of a big, old tree,

small and huge, wild and soft, a conqueror. The vibe is always right—the

magic never goes away. On my bed or in my bathroom, that's where I'll

always be found!

Maria Conchita Alonso

121

*W*hen first approached about this project, Tammy was very excited to be included, as she took great pride in our wonderful home. She personally decorated almost every room in the house, and her magic touch is everywhere. Tragically, I lost my beloved Tammy before the project could be completed, therefore, the room descriptions are my own and may not do justice to them.

Tammy and I purchased this home, originally owned by Hank Williams Sr., in 1991. It took two years of remodeling before we finally were able to move into our master suite, the centerpiece of which is an 8-foot-wide waterbed on a raised platform. Tammy always loved the feel of ceiling fans in the many tropical locales where we vacationed over the years, so we installed a ceiling fan above the bed to perpetuate that wonderful feeling. The master bath is a perfect retreat from the day-to-day worries of the world with its luxurious black marble and gold furnishings. Tammy felt like a princess in this room.

An avid collector of crystal, Tammy was especially fond of the Lalique dish where she kept about 10 cents worth of cotton that she picked in 1976 from the farm where she was born and raised. She laughingly said she hoped that would be the last cotton she ever picked…and it was! Another one of Tammy's favorite belongings was the magnificent Remington bronze statue that we enjoyed so much.

The Great Room, 45 feet by 45 feet with a vaulted ceiling, is a very warm, wonderful place to entertain or just relax. Tammy and I spent many an evening in that room playing piano and singing gospel songs with our friends. Some of my favorite memories occurred in this room; her angelic voice lifted to the rafters as I accompanied her on the grand piano.

Just off the Great Room is the formal dining room. The oriental vases and screens were some of Tammy's most cherished possessions; she would scream like a child at Christmas whenever I would find a new one for her. Another example of her extensive crystal collection is the 36-inch-tall antique crystal vase displayed in the formal living room. The delicacy of its carving is almost overshadowed by the sheer enormity of its size.

This house is so "Tammy." She did it all, and I love it all…

George Richey

In Loving Memory of *Tammy Wynette*

*W*elcome to the house The Wonder Years *bought.*

When we moved into our house, I decided that I wanted to decorate one of the rooms. I chose the dining room. I don't know why, maybe it was because it reminded me of my mom's great meals. Maybe it was because you always share great meals with friends. Oh, and it had to be a green dining room. It's my favorite color.

My wife, Eileen, designed our living room. Since the family room looks into this room, she wanted to find sofas that were a little interesting, so that we wouldn't be looking at just the back of a couch. So Eileen searched 'til she found what you see now. They have that open, airy look that lets the wood merge with the floral screen in the corner.

Eileen loves flowers and gardening. I planted a row of roses in our backyard so she would always have flowers. Those are her white roses on the table and you can see she sneaked a few into my dining room and the family room also.

The family room is where we really live. We're always watching a film by Jimmy Stewart (my favorite), Cary Grant (Eileen's favorite), William Powell, Tyrone Power, Spencer Tracy, or Katharine Hepburn, to name a few. The bookshelves are filled with old, classic movies.

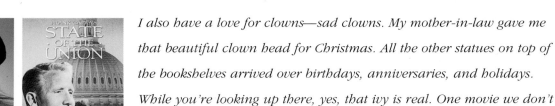

I invite many of the young actors I work with to come over, have some popcorn, watch, and learn (and steal) from some of the best actors and directors of the '30s, '40s, and '50s. They become aware of the effects of the camera angles and lighting, and how to leave the camera alone to draw the audience in (and for minimal editing).

I also have a love for clowns—sad clowns. My mother-in-law gave me that beautiful clown head for Christmas. All the other statues on top of the bookshelves arrived over birthdays, anniversaries, and holidays. While you're looking up there, yes, that ivy is real. One movie we don't watch too often is Little Shop of Horrors.

Dan & Eileen Lauria

y New York home is like an eagle's nest perched on top of a brownstone building's roof. Like a bird, I have an overlook up to the horizon to the east, with a view of the Queensboro Bridge. From the other windows and the terrace, Manhattan shows some of its famous features: the Chrysler building, the Empire State Building, and the Citibank building.

I often work on the new collections in my study. Looking up through its windows, I have direct contact with the evening stars. At night, I can feel the spirit of a never-forgotten star, Marilyn Monroe, who once lived below in apartment #13A.

This little penthouse has the spirit of a Parisian painter's atelier. The ruling colors are inspired by the artists Henri Matisse and Ferdinand Leger. The aurae of different French designers and artists from the '20s, '30s, '40s, and '50s surround me. My favorites are the paintings of Tamara de Lempika and the French furniture designs of Charlotte Perignand, Jean Prouve, Jean Royere, and

Serge Mouille. I also love the wooden sculptures of the mysterious and still undiscovered Alexandre Noll. The young and sexy American artist Jeff Koons adds a strong statement with his kitschy Cupidos sculptures over the fireplace.

Like a dinner table surrounded by artists, my rooms are filled with contradictions. My New York apartment is a constant source of inspiration, and I don't foresee a time when it will ever be finished.

129

One of my favorite things to do is decorate! When Robb, my fiancé, and I first moved into this two-story

house, we had the opportunity to start from scratch, and we loved it! We wanted the feel of our home to be

warm, loving, and romantic. What attracted us the most was the beautifully colored

old brick fireplace and the high, open, exposed beamed ceilings.

I began upstairs in the bedroom, with a wooden, eastern king, four-post canopy bed

with lots of mismatched pillows, black velvet duvet, and draped chiffon curtains—all

of which I designed and sewed by hand. On the walls we have a number of nude

paintings by artists such as Matisse, Picasso, and Degas. We love to read, so we found

a quiet corner in the bedroom and put in a chaise lounge that's wide and comfy. The

natural wooden armoire is filled with books, a stereo, and a television. I took the door

off of my closet and put up more chiffon curtains that matched the canopy and made

it into a private dressing room, where you'll find racks of clothing and my favorite

leopard stiletto heels, which express my wild side. The house has three bathrooms that

are all individualized, each with a tiled vanity and, of course, tons of candles.

Downstairs in the living room you'll find statues and art, which we've collected from

all around the world. We wanted big, fluffy, comfortable couches with mismatched

patterns. I've always enjoyed the rustic look and wrought iron, so I had the candle

holders and coffee table made out of it. In the kitchen, patio, and dining area, I've

placed big ivy plants and ficus trees; with the right lighting they illuminate and cast

shadows on the walls. Our dining room table is made out of an old Mexican church door; the legs are

ox yolks. We put a thick piece of glass over it and it has become quite the

conversation piece. The hand-painted, gold leaf mirror is from Italy and was

a gift that livens up the entire area.

We love our home, it truly is…our safe haven!

Traci Bingham

Our house is usually brimming over with kids, dogs, and music, and rarely looks like something you'd want to photograph! When we first purchased this home, it was in a 1960s Japanese style. Before we moved in, with the help of our friend, designer Maura Neilsen Kaplan, we completely changed the feel, removing the stairway's wrought-iron handrail, massive crystal chandelier, black slate entryway, and mirrors that seemed to be everywhere. We made it warm, eclectic, and funky using color in a way we never had before. We love our home!

My office is a place where I remember the past and create the future by surrounding myself with pictures of friends and family, mementos from work, and models of sets from shows I've directed; I feel I can create new lives and worlds at my desk. It's also a place where my kids know that Daddy is supposed to have total freedom from interruption. But that never works, so basically, the kids have total freedom to play games on my computer. Hey…I guess that's why they call it a home office.

Our Big Sky Carver Bear fetish started when we were living in the mountains of Park City, Utah. We still have our home there, but the ever-growing bear family came with us to Los Angeles as a reminder of clear skies, beautiful mountains, and snow on the 4th of July. The button collection began when we both were kids, Karla's favorite being "Draft Twiggy." All our watercolors were

painted by artist and longtime family friend Sylvia Sherman. We love art from children's books and have work by William Joyce and Wendy Anderson Halperin. But our favorite piece is the original Beast pencil drawing from Disney's Beauty and the Beast *by* animator Glen Keane. I worked in partnership with Glen to create the very being of this character, and will cherish his drawing and the kind words he wrote to me as much as anything in my career.

Robby Benson & Karla DeVito

135